FIVE YEARS IN UNKNOWN JUNGLES

FOR GOD AND EMPIRE

FIVE YEARS IN UNKNOWN JUNGLES

FOR GOD AND EMPIRE

Being an Account of the Founding of the Lakher Pioneer Mission, its Work Amongst (with Manners, Customs, Religious Rites and Ceremonies of) a Wild Head-hunting Race of Savage Hillsmen in Further India, Previously unknown to the Civilized World

REGINALD A. LORRAIN

GYAN

Published by

Gyan Publishing House
5, Ansari Road
Daryaganj, New Delhi-110002
Phone: 011-47034999, 9811692060
E-mail: books@gyanbooks.com

Distribution Network
gyanbooks.com
India, USA, Canada, UK, Australia, France

ISBN: 978-81-212-9300-6 (PB)
First Published, 1912

2nd Impression 2023

Printed at: Gyan Press, Delhi.

FIVE YEARS IN UNKNOWN JUNGLES FOR GOD AND EMPIRE
Author: REGINALD A. LORRAIN

FIVE YEARS IN UNKNOWN JUNGLES

FOR GOD AND EMPIRE

MR. REGINALD A. LORRAIN.

The Author and Pioneer to the Wild Head-hunting tribes of Lakher-land.

Frontispiece.]

FIVE YEARS IN UNKNOWN JUNGLES

FOR GOD AND EMPIRE

Being an account of the Founding of the Lakher Pioneer Mission, its work amongst (with Manners, Customs, Religious Rites and Ceremonies of) a wild Head-hunting Race of Savage Hillsmen in Further India, previously unknown to the Civilized World

By

REGINALD A. LORRAIN

WITH TWENTY-NINE UNIQUE HALF-TONE ILLUSTRATIONS FROM PHOTOGRAPHS TAKEN BY THE AUTHOR, AND ONE MAP

SECOND EDITION

LONDON
LAKHER PIONEER MISSION
23, BURGOYNE ROAD, SOUTH NORWOOD, S.E.

To

MAUD LOUISE LORRAIN (NÉE ULANDER)

THE LOVING AND DEVOTED WIFE OF THE AUTHOR,
WHO THROUGH ALL THE TRIALS AND HARDSHIPS
OF PIONEERING THE WILD TRIBES OF LAKHER
AND IN MOTHERHOOD HAS EVER BORNE
A SMILING FACE AS A GOOD
SOLDIER OF JESUS CHRIST;

AND THEN TO MY

BELOVED MOTHER,

THIS BOOK IS DEDICATED.

PREFACE

IN the month of July of the present year, at Keswick, I made the acquaintance of Mr. Reginald A. Lorrain, the author of this book.

It was then my privilege, at the close of the Convention, to preside at a public meeting which was held in the Victoria Hall, to hear an address from him on the Lakher Pioneer Mission.

Never shall I forget the deep interest with which I listened to Mr. Lorrain, as he narrated the history of an enterprise whose Christian devotion recalls even the ministry of the Apostles.

It is, therefore, with peculiar pleasure that I comply with Mr. Lorrain's request to write a brief Preface to the following pages.

The book will speak for itself, and will win for its author the confidence which he richly merits, and the sympathetic co-operation and financial help which the Lakher Pioneer Mission requires.

We all admire the great Missionary Societies and the noble men and women who, from time to time, go forth under their auspices. But I have a special admiration for Mr. and Mrs. Lorrain, who went forth into the "regions beyond" without being connected with any Society, but, on the contrary, trusting entirely in the Lord for their daily support, as well as for spiritual blessing upon their work.

Mr. Lorrain's narrative reads like a romance.

The Divine call, received in loyal surrender and obedience, followed by Divine leading, Divine protection, Divine supply and Divine victory—these incidents stand out upon the pages with surprising clearness and captivating interest.

When we remember that the Lakher Pioneer Mission is only five years old; that, during that time the language of the people has been reduced to writing; that a grammar and dictionary, a primer and hymn-book have been compiled; and that the Gospel according to St. John has been translated, and the process of printing by the British and Foreign Bible Society is now completed—when we remember these things, we may well exclaim: "What hath God wrought!"

I commend this book to the Christian public. It will not only obtain well-merited help for the Lakher Pioneer Mission, but it will also strengthen faith in "the glorious Gospel," in the power of the Holy Spirit, and in the over-ruling and all-pervading providence of God.

JAMES MOUNTAIN, D.D.

St. John's Manse,
Tunbridge Wells, *November*, 1912.

CONTENTS

ILLUSTRATIONS

All the above illustrations (with the exception of the four marked *) are from photos taken by the author in Lakherland.

FIVE YEARS IN UNKNOWN JUNGLES

FOR GOD AND EMPIRE

CHAPTER I

THE BUGLE CALL

SILENTLY but surely the years of time are slipping by. The sand glass of life which for each individual has at one time a starting, is rapidly sinking towards its close. White, brown, yellow, red, or whatever colour the skin, by whatever name the Nation is known, all are passing through time into the great Eternity beyond, and yet " Does nobody care ? " " Does nobody care ? " the Eternal Destiny of the millions of suffering humanity, is it nothing to those who live in a country called Christian ?

Such were the thoughts that continually ran through my mind year in and year out when as a lad sitting on the school form my mind especially turned to the peoples of the Amazon and to the peoples of Africa. In after life God led me forth into the Western Hemisphere, there to spend four years in Colonial life of hardship and variety of service that proved to be my college course for the future work of my life.

Returning to England in October, 1902, with the firm intention of endeavouring to go forth into the Mission field should the way open, I did all in my power to persuade some Missionary

Society to send me forth. But the way was closed to myself, and for three years I was doomed to remain in a London office.

Having been engaged to be married for a number of years, and every effort to go into the Mission field having failed, I decided that all my efforts with regard to the Mission field should be thrown on one side, that I should get married and settle down comfortably, and having come to this decision I abandoned the thought of a Missionary's career and made arrangements to settle down to a life of business in London.

Not long after this decision had been reached, on going one day from one room to another, something very distinctly seemed to speak to me. My thoughts had not been filled of late with Mission work, and as far as I am aware my thoughts were turned towards other matters at the time. But I had these thoughts given to me distinctly and clearly :—"Write a pamphlet on the tribes of Further India and have it inserted in the ——— Magazine."

Whatever one may think or believe, to me this voice proved the very Voice of God, and so much did these thoughts impress me that I immediately returned to my bedroom, and getting down on my knees I offered a prayer similar to the following :—

> "*Lord God, if that was Thy voice speaking to me bidding me go out to Further India as the ambassador of Thy Word, on my rising from my knees and taking my Bible and opening it at random, will Thou give me a confirmation of that voice, and if Thou dost give me a confirmation I will go.*"

After this short prayer I rose from my knees, walked over to the dressing table, and taking up my Bible let it open in my hand at random, and my eyes immediately fell on the 16th to 20th verses of the 10th Chapter of St. Luke. Especially was my attention called to the 16th, 18th and 19th verses :—

> *"He that heareth you heareth Me ; and he that despiseth you despiseth Me ; and he that despiseth Me despiseth Him that sent me. And He said unto them, I beheld Satan as lightning fall from Heaven. Behold I give unto you power to tread on serpents and scorpions and over all the power of the enemy : and nothing shall by any means hurt you."*

This happened on the 11th day of February, 1905, and could there be a more distinct confirmation of the Voice of God than the confirmation which He had given to me. "If Thou wilt give me the confirmation I will go!" in my prayer I had promised. The confirmation had come. There was nothing more for me to do than to take God at His word and go forward.

Further India was to be the field of my labour. Why, I knew not. I was sure of the call. I was sure of the field. I was sure of God's Blessing.

My brother, J. Herbert Lorrain, who had been working independently amongst the "Abor" tribes of Northern India, had been asked by the Baptist Missionary Society to return to the country of his first pioneering labours in Lushai and had done so, and the Abor field had been abandoned only on the promise that another Missionary would be sent up there. This promise had not been kept as far as I knew, and my mind immediately reverted to the Abor work which my brother had left, and I felt that it was probable that God was calling me to continue that work. Sitting down, I wrote to my brother a long letter, stating to him the facts which I thought necessary for the occasion, telling him of my definite call to the field and mentioning that it must be the Abor work that I was called to undertake.

In due time I had his reply, which stated that almost by the same post that brought my letter to him, another letter had arrived mentioning that the American Baptist Missionary Society were sending up a missionary to the Abor country to carry on the work which he had pioneered. This of course closed the door to myself, but in the same letter my brother mentioned the great needs of a wild tribe of head-hunting hillsmen which lay seven days' journey south of their present station, and who were known as the "Lakhers," and for whom the Christian natives in Lushai had been very definitely praying for some time past, that a Missionary might be sent to tell these wild people of the Love of God and of His Son, Jesus Christ.

On receiving this letter and making it a matter of prayer I decided that the Lakher country was evidently the sphere of labour to which the Lord had called, and for whom every endeavour must be made to reach.

There was very little inducement in the field of labour, for the country lay practically a month's journey from civilization, and our Mission station would have to be made some seven days' journey from the nearest white man, who would be my own brother, and the same distance from a post office. The language had never been reduced to writing, was unknown to the civilized world, and the people lay as a raw, heathen tribe in the midst of the dense jungle of extreme Further India.

I started to work with much prayer and meditation. The first pamphlet was written, and I wrote for permission to have it inserted between the leaves of the magazine which I had distinctly heard in my call, and permission was immediately granted, the leaflet was circulated with the magazine and I myself started to interest friends in the proposed work of the PIONEER MISSION TO THE LAKHERS. My first idea was to endeavour to get one of the large Missionary Societies to undertake the work, and I put forward the claims of these Lakhers to two of our present leading societies, but both applications were refused. I then tried to obtain help from the then new Arthington Trust in three of its different branches, but from none of them could I obtain the slightest help in my endeavour to reach these needy people. Each society found it impossible to extend their work to this far remote region, although they had some half million of money in their hands apiece, from the Arthington Trust for work identical to that, whose claims I placed before them. One society informed me that on consideration they might accept myself for a missionary and send me to whatever part of the world they wished, and refuse Lakher-Land as a field, or on the other hand they might accept Lakher-Land as a field and refuse me as their Missionary, to which I felt bound to reply that they must either accept the Lakher field and myself or else they must leave both myself and the Lakher field alone.

Finding that all help as far as Societies were concerned was out of the question, feeling sure that God had called, and that if the Missionary Societies shut their ears to the cry of the dying Lakhers, God was both able and willing to perform the work in other ways, I immediately set to work to interest all the people I could in the proposed work, with the view of going out independent of any existing society, trusting that the Lord would give us the support needed.

It was, however, soon placed upon my mind that in going to a far distant land and to such an out-of-the-way spot of the globe, it was necessary and wise that one should have some medical training before entering upon such an enterprise. After definite prayer I decided that it was God's will that I should enter Livingstone College at the beginning of the year's course, which started in the following October, and to put off my marriage and going forth into the field for another twelve months.

How to find the money necessary to go through Livingstone College was the next consideration, and after much prayer, believing that God meant me to take this step, I was still unable to see my way clear. The time came, however, when within a week I should have to resign my position in London if I wished to enter the College course at the commencement, which I believed was my right step to take. Day by day went by, yet there was no light thrown upon the future. At last Friday night came, and on the next morning I should have to send in my resignation if I wished to enter the College at the proper date. Friday night was much spent in prayer, and on Saturday morning I went down to my breakfast in a very undecided frame of mind, almost determined to send in my resignation and yet not feeling sure whether it would be right for me to do so or not.

On entering into the room where my breakfast was laid I found on my plate a letter in a strange handwriting. I opened this letter and out fell a cheque for £45 to help me towards my Livingstone College course, and this cheque was from a stranger whom I had never met nor knew, save for a few lines which had been written to me a few days before asking one or two off-hand questions in regard to the proposed Mission, and this cheque which I held in my hand made God's Will perfectly clear to me, so on arriving at business I sent in my resignation and in due course entered Livingstone College.

In many a wonderful way God helped me to complete that medical course, raising up friends to help at a time of need, and in due time walking the hospitals became a thing of the past and greater things lay ahead.

Some time after I was informed by the lady who had sent this cheque for £45 that she had heard of the Mission through the circular I had written and inserted in the magazine, and that the circular came as a clear answer to prayer, for she had been praying for some long time past that the Lord would give her an absolutely new pioneer work in which to interest herself for His Glory. So God answers prayer.

While the Lord was directing our steps in England He was preparing our way in India. At the time that these things happened one could not see the working of the Lord in them, but in looking back over the past years very distinctly and clearly can the workings of the Lord be seen in reference to the Salvation of His Lakher people. "God moves in a mysterious way His wonders to perform. He plants His footsteps on the sea and rides upon the storm."

A band of wild Lakher hillsmen from a village known as Zongling chased a family of slaves who had escaped and crossed into British territory. They captured them on British ground and forcibly carried them back to their village over the border, and taking the father of the family they strung him up to a tree, and thus his life was lost. The little incident in itself does not seem to amount to very much, but because these slaves had been taken from British territory across the border it necessitated the British Government sending an expedition to this village to punish these people in order that the prestige of the British Government might be upheld. In order that the expedition should be sent into the country, some kind of road along the terrible precipices had to be cut, and immediately operations were set in hand and a little political path two feet in width, just wide enough for a pony to crawl along, was cut, the whole seven days' journey to the very spot where the new Mission station was to be situated. Without this road it would have been an enormous task to have ever reached the country at all, but God saw the need, and in His marvellous way He directed the steps of all concerned. The Government, however, took practically two years before they sent this punitive expedition to punish the Lakhers for this offence, and ere the expedition arrived the Mission station was established by us on the extreme frontier and only twelve miles from the village that was to be punished. I just mention this to show the wonderful way in which God moves and that all things work together for good although at the time we may not see it, yet when we cast a glance over the years that have gone by we can see the finger prints of the Lord in all the ways.

Not only through the above incident was the Lord opening up the way for His Word, but in August, 1905, a letter written on a scrap of paper was received by my brother at Lungleh with a request for the Gospel. The writer was the son of a Lakher Chief who had previously for a few months had occasion to be in Lungleh, and while there came under the sound influence of the Gospel message and learned a little of the Lushai language and how to read and write a little in it.

Below we give a reproduction of the actual letter, and the translation following will speak for itself.

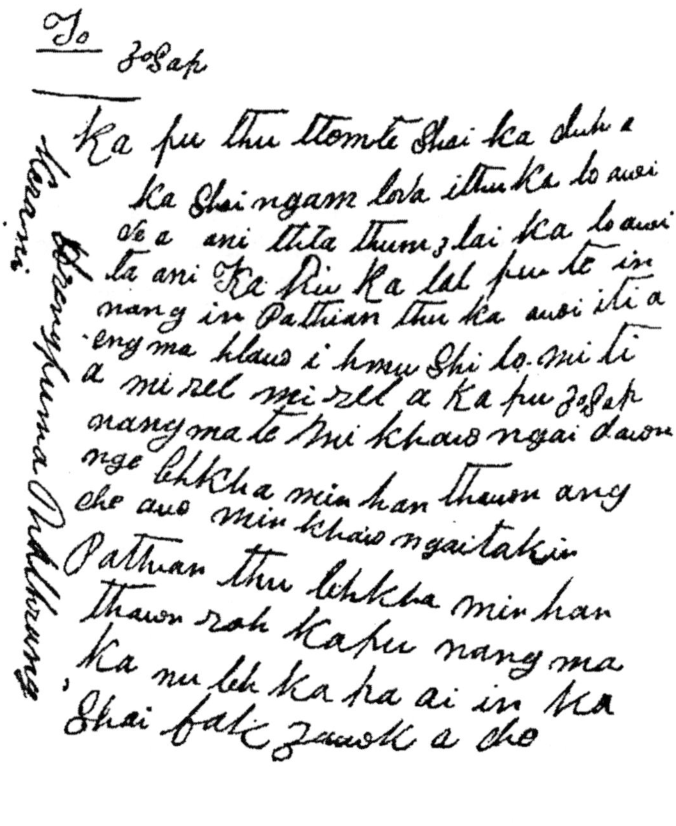

To Zosap

Ka pu thu ttomte Shai ka duh a
Ka Shai ngam lova ithu ka lo awi
ve a ani ttila thum3 lai ka lo awi
la ani Ka Riu Ka lal pu te in
nang in Pathian thu ka awi iti a
eng ma hlaus i hmu Shi lo. mi ti
a mi rel mi rel a Ka pu Zosap
nang ma te Mi khaw ngai daw
nge lehkha min han thawn ang
che aw min khaw ngaitakin
Pathian thu lehkha min han
thawn roh Ka pu nang ma
Ka nu leh ka pa ai in ka
Shai fak zawk a che

[illegible]

[TRANSLATION.]

Received at FORT LUNGLEH,
August, 1905.

To THE LUSHAI SAHIB,
[My Grandfather]

I want to say a few words but I hardly dare say them. I also have become obedient to your word. It is now three months or thereabout since I first believed. My fellow chiefs are constantly speaking against me, and they are trying to make me think that if I obey God's word I shall gain nothing by it. My Grandfather, the Lushai Sahib, you I know will sympathize with me; will you kindly send me a letter and also a book containing God's words? My Grandfather, you are more to me than my Mother and Father.

Hrengpuma,
Phalhrung Village.

Addressed to—

SERKAWN VILLAGE, to be given to
My Grandfather, the Lushai Sahib.

In calling us forth, in opening the way and in preparing the hearts of these wild head-hunting tribes for the message of Salvation the Lord was most wonderfully leading us into the heart of the unknown that His Name might be glorified.

CHAPTER II

THE UNKNOWN LAND

LAKHER-LAND is a country far remote from civilization in extreme Further India, being bordered on the north by Assam, on the south by Arakan, on the east by Burma. Practically the whole of the Lakher country covers a large area of the North Arakan Yoma Mountains, and while the countries which border Lakher-Land come under the British flag, Lakher-Land itself does not own allegiance to any Government, but is ruled entirely by its own Chiefs, presiding over their own villages, with the exception of a few Lakher villages on the Assam frontier who own in some slight measure allegiance to the Assam Government, and the Lakher Pioneer Mission Station is built on the extreme frontier amongst these Lakhers.

The country consists of range upon range of rugged mountains, ranging from 3,000 to 5,000 feet above the sea level, save for one mountain which stands out very prominently throughout the whole of the country, its peak rising to an altitude of 7,100 feet, and is known on the maps as the "Blue" mountain, its name probably being derived from the hazy blue colour that it often appears to have when viewed at a great distance. The whole country seems to be the outcome of some gigantic volcanic disturbance in ages past, for the ruggedness of the country can in no slight measure be imagined by those who have never visited or travelled along these mountain ranges. Huge precipices in some places amounting to probably 2,000 feet in depth, in other places 100 feet in depth, are very numerous, and where actual precipices do not occur, the slopes of the hillsides are so enormously steep that for a white man it is a most tedious task to either descend or ascend, the boots often slipping and precipitating one on the ground. The native paths over these mountains are of the most primitive and generally consist of following a water course, which is of necessity filled with huge boulders, and the continual climbing over these large rocks, not to say anything about the numerous times that one goes one yard ahead and two yards back to find one's self sitting down in a pool of water may be, is extremely fatiguing.

The Lakher mode of traversing from one village to another is exceedingly simple, but for a white man to follow on the same principles is, to say the least, a risky business owing to the boots not being able to grip the ground as firmly and surely as the naked feet of the Lakhers are able to do. The Lakher villages are built on the summits of the mountains, never in the valleys, and the men of one village wishing to visit a village situated on some distant peak would make a bee line descent of their mountain side until they arrived in the valley below, where of necessity in a rugged and precipitous country like unto Lakher-Land, every valley must needs have its water course. They follow it down for miles and miles until they arrive at the foot

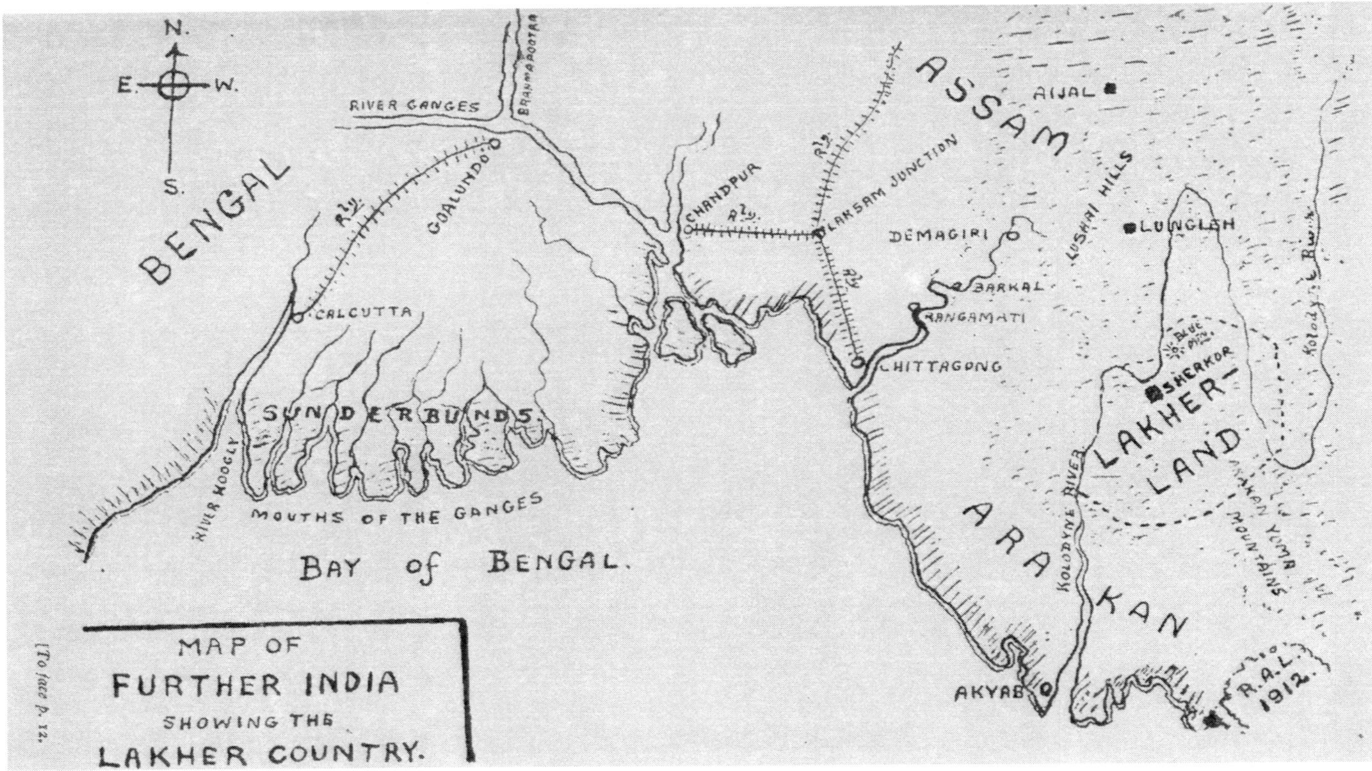
N.
E.
W.
S.
BENGAL
RIVER GANGES
BRAHMAPOOTRA
GOALUNDO
CALCUTTA
SUNDERBUNDS
RIVER HOOGLY
MOUTHS OF THE GANGES
BAY of BENGAL.
CHANDPUR
LAKSAM JUNCTION
ASSAM
AIJAL
LUSHAI HILLS
LUNGLEH
DEMAGIRI
BARKAL
RANGAMATI
CHITTAGONG
SHERKOR
LAKHER-LAND
KOLODYNE RIVER
ARAKAN YOMA MOUNTAINS
ARAKAN
AKYAB
R.A.L. 1912.
MAP OF
FURTHER INDIA
SHOWING THE
LAKHER COUNTRY.

[To face p. 12.

of the mountain on whose peak is situated the village that they wish to visit, and when opposite to the village they leave the water course and in a bee line ascend the mountain side, ultimately arriving at the desired haven. This mode of finding one's way is of course following one of the most primitive methods, but in a country where one cannot move without either going down hill or up hill and where huge precipices of gigantic size and depth are continually looming forth, such a mode of travelling as this is practically impossible for the white man who has all his life had his feet enclosed in a covering of leather.

There is practically no flat land in Lakher, even of such small dimensions as would be needed to erect a bungalow, nothing but hills and valleys, rivers and rocks, the sides of the mountains being densely covered with jungle from the foot to the brow.

In some parts this jungle consists of miles of bamboo forest, and where the bamboo occurs very little undergrowth is experienced. In other parts the jungle consists of a number of gigantic trees, with some of lesser dimensions, but the trees of Lakher are very much scarcer than they are through the country which we have to pass in order to reach Lakher, but the undergrowth is exceedingly dense. Creeping vines and small shrubs, ferns and bracken in great numbers, intermingled with various species of stinging nettles, some of which are indeed poisonous, and the sting of which, although not causing death, will give one a very unpleasant three or four days' severe illness. Poisonous vines are found in these jungles in great numbers.

I should like to mention one of these vines in

particular. It is called by the Lakher natives "I-TA-MEI" (pronounced "E-TA-MAY-E") and grows to great length, twining and intertwining itself from bamboo to bamboo or from bush to bush, and specially is it fond of throwing its tendrils across any path that is used as a public highway. Innocent enough in its looks and in the vine itself it is innocent, but at a certain season of the year it throws out its blossom not unlike the scarlet runner in construction, but each flower is nearly as big as a sweet pea, and is of such a deep violet as to almost amount to jet black, and yet it has an extremely pleasing effect to the eye.

As soon as the flowers fall off the bean-shaped fruit bearing the seed commence to form, and these grow until they attain the size of a large scarlet runner, and another species, apparently of this same plant, forms into a large, round bean not of long structure as in the other case but from two to three inches in diameter. In both of these species this bean fruit on reaching maturity becomes a rich velvety colour and looks exactly as if it were covered in velvet, but this velvety appearance is made up of hundreds of thousands of very short, fine spines, and these form the dangerous part of the creeper. When mature, the breath of the wind, the touching of some portion of the vine with one's hat or hand or stick, will cause thousands of these spines to immediately leave the bean fruit and float invisibly (so exceedingly fine are they) through the air. The moment these spines touch you they set up such an irritation all over the body that it nearly drives one mad, and its effects will last for a period of about five minutes, then you will have a rest of two to three minutes and another five minutes of this excruciating irritation, and so on throughout the course of an hour and a half to two hours until its powers are expended. Whatever one does to relieve one's self seems to be of no avail. The natives claim that smothering one's self in mud will alleviate the pain, but a white man of necessity does not care to try the experiment, even were the mud procurable, which is very often out of the question at the time, and one has to simply grin and bear it.

The old saying, however, "Once bitten, twice shy," is very applicable in this case, and when once you have had your baptism into the powers of the "I-TA-MEI" vine, needless to say you take great care to endeavour not to come into contact with those powers again.

Throughout these hills the wild Plantain Tree grows in great profusion, with its wide spreading leaves that are often very useful to the traveller, taking the place of an umbrella should a tropical storm catch him unawares during his various travels. Tea also is a native of the country, and we in England often associate the Tea Tree with a small, under-sized bush. But in its own wild state the tea plant grows to a tree of some large dimensions in so much that by the Lakhers it is called "*Tho-pi*," which means "The Gigantic Tree."

Although a native of these hills, the tea tree is not common, and one might spend the whole of one's life in the country without even seeing one were they not to search for it. But about two miles from where the Lakher Pioneer Mission station has been established there is a large area of jungle which is for the greater part a garden of tea trees, bearing a small seed enclosed in a hard, round shell which is black, and now and again a dark brown, and in size resembles a large cherry. Tea, however, from a full grown tree is not suitable for consumption.

Another very interesting tree which may be found in these hills is a species of Cotton Tree which attains to great height and large girth of trunk. This tree sheds its leaves every year, and I might mention here that very few trees in the country ever appear to shed their leaves, one or two species only ever being found bare, thus the greater part of the jungle is evergreen. When the season arrives for the cotton tree to show signs of life it first of all bursts out into flower, large red flowers which can be seen at a great distance. The flower soon drops and a pod forms, and when this pod is mature it bursts open and the contents fall to the ground, the tree afterwards bursting into leaf. Now the great usefulness of this tree is that these pods are packed with a kind of down and this can be gathered, the pods being thrown away. The down makes an excellent cushion, but in order that it shall be suitable for use it must be gathered before the pod bursts. This cotton tree down is sold on the market in this country I believe under the name of "Vegetable Down," but the country however does not abound to any large extent in these trees, and one of the great difficulties in gathering this valuable material is that in nearly every case it necessitates the felling of the tree, as the trunks are almost unclimbable, being of such great girth and height, and the upper branches rather slim.

The India-rubber Tree is also a native of this country, and in years gone by the forests used to abound in this useful product. But a number of years back the Lakhers, finding that they could get a good price (viz., guns, knives and beads) from the native traders in the south for the sap of the rubber tree, bled nearly all their trees to death, and to-day only isolated specimens of the commercial rubber may be found in the country.

The most useful of all these products of the jungle is the Bamboo, of which there are six or seven species or more ranging from the size of a very small cane to six inches in diameter. Of all these species of bamboo, the "True Bamboo" is the most useful and springs up in the jungle singly, one by one, rising from twenty to forty feet in height. The other species of bamboo occur in clumps, a number springing out from the common root, and have a much thicker wood, but these are of very little use in the construction of houses, etc., while the "True Bamboo" is invaluable.

Throughout the whole of this dense jungle many wild animals abound, from the smaller to the greater species of the animal kingdom. Jungle Wolves, or Wild Dogs; Civet Cats, in great variety; the Barking Deer; the Samber Deer; the Rhinoceros; the king of these jungles, the Tiger; and the largest animal of all, the Elephant. In greater numbers than any of the above animals appears the monkey, of which there are a number of species. The common monkey, such as we see on the organs in our English streets, abounds in these forests, the natives relishing the flesh of it greatly, and which resembles our mutton in taste, but is exceedingly rich eating. The long-tailed monkey is also found in large troops, whilst the Gibbon Ape is seen swinging from branch to branch, calling out with its weird, hollow sound. These Gibbon Apes have no tails, and are the nearest approach to human beings that I have ever seen. One thing I have noticed about these Gibbon Apes, which does not appear to be mentioned in natural history, is that the female is nearly always grey whilst the males are dark, and it is quite a picture to see these noble animals caring for their young; and there is no nicer pet that one can wish for than a young Gibbon Ape, which will soon learn to care for one and throw its arms around your neck as if it were a child.

Amongst the feathered flock many species of game are present. The Peacock Pheasant, the Black Pheasant, the Partridge and many others; also the Jungle Fowl; whilst the smaller birds from the Paroquet downwards abound on every side. Some of these birds are most beautiful to behold, being bright crimson and of various hues. There is one bird in particular whose male and female differ only in the colours of their bodies, the one being crimson and the other blue, but with all their beauty they are no songsters. The Paroquets have two long feathers in their tails, and these feathers are considered of value in the hands of a Lakher native. Numerous Eagles and Kites also abound throughout the country and make desperate raids on the domestic fowls.

In the jungle also are found several species of the Land Tortoise, running into large sizes, the flesh of which is considered a great delicacy. In the rivers a few turtles abound, but are not so numerous as are the land tortoises, whilst the waters of all the large rivers and mountain torrents abound in numbers of fish, and especially is this so at certain seasons of the year, generally during September and October, which is towards the latter end of the Rainy Season. The largest fish that it has been my lot to see was a species of Cat Fish, which was larger than a man and took two natives to carry it tied to a pole, caught in the Kolodyne River, which runs through the country, in which alligators also are found in small numbers. Many "Marseer" may be caught ten to fourteen pounds apiece in weight, but these of necessity take a good deal of skill in landing, and lucky is the angler who is fortunate enough to hook one of these large specimens if it does not cause him to lose his tackle and fail to land his catch.

CHAPTER III

OFF TO THE EAST

AFTER an endless amount of worry and toil we saw the last of our cases leave our abode, and with a sigh of relief realized that at last all our goods were packed and off on their long journey to the Indian frontier.

The morning of Friday, January 18, 1907, at last dawned. Accompanied by a number of friends my brave wife and myself made our way to Euston, where we were to say good-bye to all those we loved, and thence to go forward to Liverpool and to India, to a new life, a new country, attended with difficulties and triumphs which we had not the slightest power to imagine.

The morning was an exceedingly foggy one, for one of London's black fogs hung over the city, and although we started at an early hour, leaving several hours' grace in order that nothing should cause us to miss the train, yet we had the great disappointment of arriving at Euston within ten minutes of the departure of the Liverpool express. Quite a number of friends and relatives were gathered there to say a last few words, but we were obliged to say good-bye very rapidly and to jump into the train as she pulled out of the station, our hold-all being passed in to us whilst the train was in motion. The scream of the engine whistle, a wave of the hand from out of the window, and we passed forward into the unknown, leaving all those that we loved and who loved us standing in that thick London fog.

In due course we arrived at Liverpool and went aboard the s.s. *City of Glasgow*, and sailed out of the Mersey in the early hour of the following morning. On January 30 we arrived at Port Said, after an extremely rough, rainy and cold passage. As my wife and myself were anxious to stretch our legs on land once again, after two weeks on the water, we decided to go ashore with another missionary, his wife and their two children, who were bound for Calcutta. The night was extremely dark, so dark that one could hardly see the faces of their fellow-passengers in the little rowing boat that was taking us ashore and which was manned by a Turk. Our ship lay a long way out and the rain was pelting down upon us through that long row, making it exceedingly uncomfortable for every one concerned.

After having rowed about two-thirds of the distance between our ship and the land our boatman either ran our boat into the side of another boat, or else the other boat ran into our boat, but the night was so dark that it was impossible to be sure who was at fault. The Turkish boatman in the other boat, however, immediately seized our boatman and tried his best to get a footing into our boat. A fight ensued, which was by no means a silent one, but the only word we could understand of the whole heated quarrel was the word "Allah," which means "God," and this was repeated an enormous number of times. After a long struggle and the boats almost upsetting, and the situation becoming so serious that we were considering what we had better do to save the capsizing of our boat, our boatman seized the other man and knocked him down to the bottom of his boat, pushed off, and rowed us safely ashore. All through this unpleasant experience we had to realize that at any moment we might be hurled into the sea, and the night being so dark there would have been very little hope of rescue. Especially were we anxious on the part of the two children, but we had once more to thank God for all His mercy to us in bringing us safely through an experience which we do not wish to realize again.

On Tuesday, February 12, we arrived at Colombo, where we went ashore for two hours, and thence we sailed away through the Bay of Bengal for Calcutta, where we arrived on Saturday, February 16, and at six in the evening we were alongside the quay awaiting the rise of the water to enable us to go into the docks. It seemed hours to us as we made our way up those docks to the landing stage, where my brother (J. Herbert Lorrain) and his wife were waiting in the distance ready to give us a word of welcome, being on a visit to Calcutta in connexion with the B.M.S. Conference.

Presently the lines were thrown ashore, and slowly but surely the ship was moored alongside the dock at Kidderpore. The gangway being lowered, we were soon clasping hands with a great thankfulness in our hearts to our loving Heavenly Father for having given us a safe voyage across the mighty ocean.

Having cleared a part of our goods through the customs, the coolies soon picked up the boxes and placing them upon their heads carried them down on to the dock and placed them in a carriage which was to convey them to our night's abode. It was quite a business dealing with these coolies, and unless one keeps one's eye on them every moment it may be that the boxes will ultimately be placed into safe keeping where the Sahib will be unable to find them. After all the boxes were placed securely in and on the carriage, the man having been given directions where we were to drive to and his number being carefully noted, he drove off, while my brother and his wife and my wife and myself jumped on a tram and made our way towards the Baptist Missionary Society's House, as they had kindly consented to put us up for a few days whilst we were in Calcutta, where we found everything done for our comfort and every one was most kind.

The following morning being Sunday we went to the Baptist Church which was in the compound of the Mission House, afterwards going for a walk round the city, which seemed to us of a very mixed nature, varying from beautiful buildings and establishments to the lowest of native hovels. Sunday, however, made no difference to this city, and everything appeared to us to be in full swing amongst the native classes. It was indeed pretty to see the bullock waggons laden with rice straw and their curious drivers walking by their sides, stick in hand, calling out from time to time some words in Hindustani or other tongue in the vain hopes of hurrying the beasts along. Here and there and on every side we saw customs and people that were entirely strange to us at this time. The barber, squatting by the roadside with his client also squatting before him, whilst the operation of cutting the hair or a shave (without the slightest concern for the numbers that passed by) went on—no shop, just where you happen to meet the barber, there was his shop and tackle ready to hand. The water-carrier, with his large skin of water on his back or filling it from the hydrant by the roadside. The tailor, the tin-smith, the blacksmith, and natives of various other trades, all these were exceedingly interesting to the new-comer, whilst in between times you would find these men taking a quiet smoke from a hard kind of tobacco resembling coke, in their peculiar shaped pipes known as " Hookah." The milkman, carrying his milk in little metal jugs suspended at each end of a long bamboo pole by means of a number of strings and a ring, resembling a pair of scales, which he balances across his shoulder, is worth a moment's notice, but it is not my intention in this volume to go into details about this part of India, and therefore I simply pass over this part of the country with as few words as possible.

On the following day we were very busy in making purchases of goods to take up country with us, as from two or three days from now we should have left civilization not to behold it again for nearly five years. European stores and native shops, according to the various articles of purchase needed, were visited, and these goods being delivered and packed, that same night we left Calcutta on our long journey across country. Carriages were called, our luggage place on them, and we ourselves bade good-bye to all at the Mission House and drove off to " Sealdar Station " in good time for the train.

The noise of the coolies at this station was deafening, and double the number of coolies required would come along, catch up any small article and run off with it to the train if you were not smart enough to stop them, and a few minutes after you would have to pay for your slackness, as each man is entitled to his two pice a journey. These coolies carry an enormous weight on their heads, anything up to a hundred pounds, but one needs to keep a sharp look out on one's things. After a while, all the luggage being weighed, the excess charges having been paid on it and it had been put aboard the train, we ourselves went into our compartment. In due course the train steamed out of Calcutta, and it being late at night, we were unable to see any of the country we passed through.

Our compartment was of the second class and exceedingly comfortable, made as it was to accommodate five for sleeping, while there were only four of us and we were not troubled with any stranger during the journey. The compartment contained three long seats which could either be used as seats or as lounges, one on either side of the carriage and one in the centre longways, whilst the two side seats had a let-down bunk from the ceiling above them, the carriages of course having observation windows. At one end of the carriage was a lavatory, and by the side was the door to enter or go out of the carriage. The plan of this carriage was indeed comfortable and allowed plenty of room for luggage, of which one has a good deal when travelling in India. The seats were padded and covered with brown leather, and alongside of these carriages was a special compartment for the native servants of a European. My brother having with him two Lushai lads, whom he had brought down with him to see civilization, they occupied this compartment, and he was able to keep an eye on them and to see that no harm came to them. My wife and sister-in-law slept well for several hours, but my brother and myself preferred to keep awake, and as the train pulled up at various stations we got out and had a walk up and down the platform or along the side of the track, as many of these stations had no platform at all. At each station, however, the train was met by a large number of natives, whose hubbub appeared to be enough to wake anybody. They were selling various sweetmeats, and on stopping one of these fellows and asking him what he had to sell, he replied, "Oh, these only good for natives, no good for Sahib," and as the various mysteries on his tray did not look very tempting we did not puchase, but believed he was telling us the truth.

At about five in the morning we came to our journey's end, a place called "Goalundo," and a more miserable, dreary-looking place it is hard to imagine. There seemed to be very little else than sand in the place, and it lies on the banks of the river. I understand in the rainy season it practically disappears owing to the rise of the river, flooding the whole of this country around. Coolies very soon seized hold of our "marl" (luggage), placing the trunks and boxes on their heads and trotted off with them to the river steam-boat which was waiting for the arrival of the train. Having placed them aboard and paying them the authorized price with their dearly beloved *baksheesh* added, we were glad to get aboard and have the opportunity of getting a cup of tea, after which we laid down in our nicely furnished cabins to have an hour's rest before *chota hazarri* (little breakfast) was ready. The name of this steamer was the *Ghoorka*, and a very nice boat she was too, carrying over 1,000 passengers including all classes. These river companies are very liberal towards Missionaries, allowing them to travel first class at second-class fare, which is a great help, as it is almost impossible for a white man to travel second class on these boats.

The catering on board these vessels is very good, and the cabins are exceedingly well fitted up with a couple of couches, one on either side, with two doors, one leading on to the deck and the other leading into the dining saloon, the first class being situated afore-ship on the upper deck, and these large flat-bottomed boats are made to draw very little water.

At noon we sailed for "Chandpur," and the scenery along this river was exceedingly fine with large stretches of water on either side of us, the river being exceedingly broad and its banks covered with tropical vegetation, while here and there we could see dotted amongst the trees native villages with huts built of bamboo, and picturesque banana groves waving in the breeze helping to add greatly to the beauty and novelty of the scene. We had an enjoyable trip in company with another Missionary who had been at the B.M.S. Conference, a Mr. Hughes by name, from "Rangamuti," and who was returning to his home there.

At seven o'clock that evening we duly arrived at Chandpur, and our *marl* was again seized by coolies who trotted off with it on their heads to the railway station, where we found the train full with the exception of a first-class carriage, into which the native conductor placed us along with our luggage, but as far as we could see there was very little difference between this first-class carriage and the one we travelled in during the night before, save that this one carried only four persons and it was slightly narrower than the other compartment had been. Stowing away our luggage and making things as comfortable as possible, and finding that we had half an hour to spare, we locked up the carriage and strolled into the native market which was close at hand, there purchasing a couple of green cocoanuts and a piece of soap to wash with, and a few other useful odds and ends. At the time appointed the engine blew its whistle and our train moved out of the station on its way to "Chittagong," while my wife and self being extremely tired soon fell into a heavy slumber. When next we awoke the day was just breaking, and we were within a short run of Chittagong. We had to hastily take a wash and brush up, and then went along into the dining car to get a cup of tea and something to eat. On arriving there we found the cook fast asleep and also his boy, and we had no little trouble in waking them up. Our morning meal consisted of a cup or tea and a piece of toast, and having had nothing since six o'clock the evening before we found it very acceptable.

Arriving at Chittagong we found plenty of ox-waggons standing by in a line outside the station, and upon three of these we placed our luggage, while we ourselves jumped into a carriage and drove off several miles to the river's edge, from whose wharf we were to start our journey into the wilds of these vast hills in further India. Slowly but surely the ox-waggons laden with our *marl* jolted wearily along the road, and in due course arrived at the little wharf on the banks of the Kernaphuli river, where we had three dug-outs (small native boats which I shall describe a little later) waiting to receive this baggage and to convey it far up into the upper reaches of the Kernaphuli. We ourselves had decided to board the small steamer (*The Swallow*) for our first sixty miles' journey up the river, and which was due to leave on the early morning tide of the following day. Our three dug-outs were fastened together and the *marl* placed in the respective boats. One boat was to accommodate my brother and his wife, one boat was to accommodate my wife and myself, and the other was to be the cook boat when we should board them at Rangamuti.

At one o'clock it was the turn of the tide, and Mr. Hughes, who had travelled with us thus far, entered into his dug-out, and with our three boats, bidding us good-bye, sailed off towards his station at Rangamuti, whilst we were to follow him the next day in the steamer; and the native boatmen, to aid their progress, as well as to alleviate them from the tedious task of rowing, hoisted their sail upon one of their bamboo poles, and very soon wind and tide together took the dug-outs completely from our gaze.

The Swallow was lying at anchor a little distance from the shore. She is a small river-steamer, having two decks and only draws 4½ feet of water. She plies once a week between Chittagong and Rangamuti, when she carries passengers (both native and European) and freight. She starts from the Swallow wharf every Thursday morning by the first tide, and on the morrow she was leaving at 5 a.m. No food is served aboard. Europeans occupy the upper deck, where there are three or four cabins and a small dining saloon, its furniture consisting of a table and a few chairs, passengers bringing their own lunch along with them and serving it as they pleased, while on the lower deck there was a kitchen where a kettle could be boiled.

As it had been our desire to save the ladies as much roughness in travelling as possible, we decided to go by this little steamer as far as Rangamuti in preference to being enclosed in the little native dug-outs for two days and two nights extra. After seeing our dug-outs off we busied ourselves in visiting the native bazaar, making a few more purchases and replenishing our lunch basket, which took us until dusk, when we went aboard *The Swallow*; and after a quiet rest on deck, our thoughts going back to the Homeland and all its loved ones whom we had left five weeks before, we retired to our little cabins in the hope of a peaceful night's rest, which was to be denied us, for we found the place simply alive with tiny red ants which were swarming on everything in thousands, and wherever a crumb had fallen these little pests were busy in carrying it away. We found it quite impossible to lie or sit, or write or do anything, but let them have full sway, and we ourselves were thankful to take to the deck, while on opening our lunch basket we found that in the same condition.

The butter was covered with one mass of these little red ants; they were in the jam; as you cut your loaf of bread they teemed out of it; the sugar was full of them; the oatmeal and the condensed milk was simply besieged by them; and while one was eating one's frugal repast, one had to keep on clipping them off the side of the plate. We had taken aboard with us a square cocoa tin full of chocolate to eat while travelling. The tin had a very close lid and seemed to be air-tight, but when we opened it we found it one mass of these red ants, and were obliged to empty the chocolate all out on the deck in the heat of the sun, standing the tin there also, the only way of getting rid of these pests, as they cannot stand the sun's rays, and immediately depart in all directions. By the time the ants had departed, however, the heat of the sun had made the chocolate soft and uneatable, but we managed to save that which remained and put it into a better tin, and later on we were very pleased to have even this with us.

CHAPTER IV

LOST TO CIVILIZATION

AT 5 a.m. we weighed anchor and at 4 p.m. on the same day we should have arrived at Rangamuti, a distance of sixty miles, but we were doomed to have a longer time on board than we had anticipated or cared for. All went well until 12 noon, when we neared a sandbank that reached almost across the river, and as the water was low at this time of the year, the Sarang (native captain) must needs run our boat high and dry on this sandbank amid stream, with no chance of our floating again for twelve hours, when the tide would be high enough and the water deep enough to put us afloat once more, so we had no alternative but to resign ourselves to our fate and stay stranded on the sandbank in the middle of the river, while the red ants continued to do all they could to annoy us.

There were two other European passengers beside ourselves, and as one was only going as far as Chandragoona, three miles up the river from where we were stranded, he hailed a boat and went off in it. The other passenger was a lady who was going to Rangamuti, whose name was Mrs. Higgins, and she went ashore to see a planter for the time being.

At nine that evening the engines were started, and after much labour the boat slid over the sandbank into deep water again. The Sarang sounded the siren again and again to indicate to Mrs. Higgins that she must hurry up as we were off, and in about an hour's time Mrs. Higgins pulled alongside the steamer. She had had to run some distance and was greatly out of breath, the Sarang having told her he would not start until an hour later. To make up for lost time the Sarang promised he would run throughout most of the night as the moon was bright, and we were feeling joyful in anticipation of reaching Rangamuti by early morning, but the old adage, " You must not crow until you are out of the wood," proved very true in this case.

For three miles all went well, and we arrived at Chandragoona, a lonely Mission station on the banks of the Kernaphuli, and amongst the cargo there being a couple of boxes and a table to be placed ashore, a boat came out to mid-stream to receive these goods. The Sarang left his post to see that the freight was handed over; the two natives at the wheel also thought they would like to look on as well, and leaving their posts of duty they followed the Sarang, with the speedy result that the steamer swung round and drifted helplessly on to another sandbank which was waiting to receive her, and do what they would everything failed entirely to bring the boat afloat again, while the Sarang stood looking extremely surprised at this latest disaster; but words were of no avail, and we were doomed to resign ourselves to our fate and await the turn of the next tide, which was about 11 a.m. the following day.

We were, however, at Chandragoona, where a Dr. and Mrs. Taylor, Missionaries of the B.M.S., were stationed. The doctor very kindly came aboard and invited us all up to their bungalow, from which a lovely view could be obtained of the river winding in and out, with its banks thickly covered with jungle. On our right lay the low lands or plains, while in front and on our left lay the Chittagong Hill Tracts, and making in all a lovely view. Bidding our friends good-night, we again made our way to *The Swallow*, but when the time came for us to get afloat once more the tide did not rise high enough to accomplish the act, and so we were destined to stay another twelve hours until the following night tide.

The native sailors seemed to make a lot of noise, plenty of talking and arguing and quarrelling, but very little energy put forth in order that we might get on our journey. We asked the Sarang why he did not get us off by that tide, and he politely answered us and said, " There was not enough water," and added, " The things written on my brow are not good, they are bad." He himself was very anxious to get the trip over and arrive back at Chittagong for the following Sunday, as there was a great Mahomedan festival due, at which he wanted to be present. Had it not been for this festival we might have been on the sandbank for a few more tides to pass.

Dr. and Mrs. Taylor, on hearing of our plight—for by this time our lunch basket was getting very low, and Mrs. Higgins not having brought anything with her, put in her lot with us—kindly invited us all up to spend the rest of the day with them, for which we were very thankful, and we again wended our way up the steep hillside that took us to their bungalow. A few days before this, on this very path, a native on passing by spied a tiger sitting close beside the path, and he very foolishly took up a large clod of earth and threw it full at the tiger's face. The animal's savage nature was immediately aroused, and springing upon the man it tore his arm from his shoulder and made off into the jungle. Had the poor man not have been so foolish as to have infuriated the animal, he might have passed safely by.

Late that evening we returned to *The Swallow*, and we saw at once that unless we kept very close to the Sarang's side we should not be off that sandbank that night, so we took the sounding lines and sounded for him, and in this way we knew exactly how many feet of water there were in the tide.

It was simply appalling to see the amount of energy those natives put into their work. With the tide almost on the turn, and in ten or fifteen minutes all power to move the boat would be beyond any of us, those fellows stood jabbering to one another, watching the boat instead of putting forward any energy to get it off. We needed 5 feet of water to allow our boat to float, and it was a seven-foot tide. With an enormous amount of persuasion and "edging on" we at last managed to get the Sarang to work up sufficient energy in his sailors to hoist the vessel off the sandbank by means of a cable and capstan.

During this operation one little adventure is worth recording. It was a beautiful night, the stars shining brightly in the sky, and the moon shedding her soft rays across the river. The cable was attached to a tree on the bank, while the other end of it was round our capstan. With a merry chatter of voices the native sailors were winding the cable in, and which was strained to its uttermost, when at a short distance we spied a dug-out coming along the river between our ship and the shore. In the bow were two men rowing, aft was the Margie (head boatman) steering. Another native was sitting perched on the top of the bamboo covering, evidently with his thoughts far away, or else he must have been star-gazing. On they came at full speed, heedless of our shouts, the native still squatting calmly on the top of the bamboo roof. The next moment the boat passed under our cable, but it was sufficiently high to miss the heads of the rowers, and scraping along the roof of the boat it caught the man who was sitting on the top, who, turning a somersault, found himself flying into the river. Fortunately for him he was not hurt, and as his only raiment was a loin cloth and a blanket he had not much to get wet. All the same he no doubt enjoyed the cold bath in the middle of the night far more than we should have done ourselves.

At last the cable tugged our steamer from off the sandbank and we slid once more into deep water, and putting on full steam ahead we were very thankful to arrive at about ten o'clock the following morning at Rangamuti.

Of course Mr. Hughes had arrived a long time before ourselves, and our three luggage boats were tied up to the bank awaiting our arrival. We had promised to stay with Mr. Hughes for a day or two, but owing to the delay on the journey we were unable to fulfil that promise, and after breakfasting with them and laying in a stock of loaves to last us for the next nine or ten days, as we were leaving bakers far behind, we made our way to our little dug-outs and, bidding Mr. and Mrs. Hughes good-bye, sailed away towards the upper reaches of the river.

Our men rowed till very late that night, ultimately arriving at "Kassalong." Here alongside the bank of the river we tied up for the night and for the following day, it being Sunday.

Kassalong is a little village comprised of a few native houses in the dense jungle and not visible from the river, but the place was full of interest for us, as it was here that my brother and his colleague nearly died of fever and want of food some twelve years before, when they were endeavouring to enter the Lushai country in order that they might carry the Word of God to those then notorious Head-Hunters, a similar Mission to that which my wife and myself were undertaking at the present time. We visited the old site where their little bungalow had stood, but no trace remained save a little cleared spot in the jungle which marked its whereabouts and the little footpath leading from the river's bank up to it.

On our journey up the river both banks had been thickly covered with jungle, where numerous troops of monkeys were continually seen sporting in the trees and making no end of noise. Parrots, too, with gay plumage, fluttered about and gave us much interesting study. Needless to say, the sun beamed down on us with all its power, and we found it at times intensely hot.

Very early the following morning our boatmen took us forward again on our journey, and the water being exceedingly shallow in this part—this being the height of the dry season—they found it easier to tow these little dug-outs than to row them for many miles of this day's journey. I myself got out of the boat and made my way through the jungle, cutting off a curve of the river.

On this little excursion I came across a herd of Bison belonging to a native village, but these huge creatures looked so unfriendly towards me that I thought it best to avoid their company, and I had a difficult task in climbing over many large boulders in order to pass them at a safe distance. After this experience I found myself very much fatigued and decided to wend my way to the river's bank, which I accomplished with much difficulty, and on the arrival of our boats, was glad to get aboard once again.

In due course we arrived at Barkal Rapids, at the foot of which we had to unload our boats, take the goods over on a trolley to the upper reaches of the river and load up new boats. Santal coolies here took our baggage and trotted it up a steep path, and placing it on a little trolley at the top, awaited our arrival. Here we experienced a heavy shower of rain, but it was soon over, and we were none the worse for its cooling beneficence. We paid off our boatmen, and with a little additional *baksheesh* they returned to their boats contented. At the little station we found a trolley to hold two people, and as there were four of us the Mem-Sahibs occupied the seats, while my brother and myself stood behind, and all four of us were pushed along by two Santal coolies, who were fine-looking men with very dark skins.

Three other trolleys were laden with our *marl*, and each of these were pushed by two Santals in the same manner, while on the top of the goods sat the two Lushai boys who were with my brother, evidently enjoying themselves and the new experiences of the journey. This track is one and a quarter mile long and runs to the head of the rapids. The cars run very smoothly, and we soon found ourselves at the upper end of the rapids where our dug-outs were awaiting us and needed loading with all speed as night was drawing on and we wished to get well on our journey.

Barkal Rapids is an extremely pretty and interesting place at this time, the water being at its very lowest. A great number of rocks appear and the noise of the water dashing upon these rocks and the roaring of the torrent is very fascinating.

Up to the present I have omitted to mention the nature of these dug-outs. A dug-out is the hollowed out trunk of a large tree with the ends running almost to a point, and is probably between 35 and 40 feet in length. Its widest part, which is the centre of the boat, would be approximately 4½ feet. A boat of this description will draw about 6 inches of water when not laden. The centre of this boat is dug out—thus its name—leaving a shell of about 2 inches in thickness which forms the hull of the boat. Two hoods comprised of bamboo matting then covers the boat from stem to stern, leaving a space in the centre between them of about 2 feet, where from the floor of the boat to the top of the hood it is practically 4 feet, and under these coverings one has to spend the greater part of one's day and night, only being able to enter into the boat in a crouching position. The highest part of these hood coverings is towards the centre of the boat, and they gently slope down towards the ends of the boat where they are abruptly cut off at about a height of 3 feet from the boat flooring.

At one end under this covering the Margie, or Head Boatman, sleeps. At the further end of the boat under the other covering the two rowers sleep. On the outside of this bamboo matting hood roof are three very long bamboo poles used by the men for poling the boat up the rapids or steering it between the rocks. Two rowing oars and one large steering oar comprise the machinery. Each boat is manned by three men, the Margie or Head man, who attends to the steering, and his two native rowers, who squatting in the bows of the boat ply their single oar apiece at a steady rate hour after hour.

These men are very good-tempered, and if the *baksheesh* is only sufficient, they are often quite willing to row all day and almost all the night in order to shorten the time of the journey which has so many discomforts.

Let us crawl into our dug-out and explore the interior. We find the floor consists of bamboo, with six feet either end of the boat taken up for the boatmen's beds. The rest of the boat is to be used for luggage, or if there are passengers aboard, for luggage, and passengers' sleeping accommodation. In order to make it more private, we take a blanket and hang it across the back of the men's compartment at either end. Then we pile in a sufficient amount of our luggage, leaving six feet for our own beds, on which we shall have to sleep at night and sit during the day. Then comes the two feet space in between the two hood coverings which is floored by a plank of wood, and if one is unlucky enough in going up the rapids to ship a sea it is the only place available for bailing the water out.

We then get under the next cover, and already having placed the blanket at the head of the boatmen's beds for privacy's sake, we commence piling up our luggage in the space at our command. Here we also have to put our food supply, and with a piece of bent wire hooked into the hood covering we hang up our lantern, the only means we have of light at night.

After turning in for the night the open space between these two hoods is easily covered up by a loose bamboo mat which is pulled across, thus making the situation as comfortable as possible, and would no doubt not be so bad were it not for the myriads of mosquitos, sand-flies and other tiny pests that all unite together with the determination not to let one have much sleep; and although it is an extremely awkward place to fasten up a mosquito net, unless one take this precaution it will probably mean forfeiting one's sleep.

The only way to describe the elaborate accommodation that is supplied in these boats is by likening it to living under a dining room table for a week or ten days. One, however, can climb on the roof, and sitting down can enjoy the scenery, save for the terrific heat of the sun. Inside the boat one must either squat down or lie down, and the dressing ordeal is perhaps the most awkward of any. We take the precaution of placing in these boats under the bottom of our bed our waterproof ground sheet, a very necessary precaution as we found out, for in going up the rapids in the upper reaches we shipped many a sea, and had we not taken this precaution should have had to sleep in wet blankets. A camp tidy hung up on the side of the wall, containing comb and brush, looking-glass, towel, soap, etc., we found to be most useful.

On the roof at the further end of the boat is an old kerosine oil tin which forms the fireplace, and the fire is made by means of pieces of dry bamboo. On this primitive fireplace the kettle has to be boiled and all the cooking done.

Every night we tied up to the bank of the river alongside of the jungle; the men, making large fires, cooking their evening meal over these fires, afterwards sitting round them for an hour or so, having a quiet smoke at their *hookahs*, would spend the time in spinning a few camp stories, after which tumbling into their beds at the ends of the dug-outs would sleep soundly until just before daybreak, when they start off again.

On the upper reaches of this river the scenery was simply lovely. At intervals we would come across little islands thickly covered with long grass and looking extremely picturesque as we passed between them. The river wound in and out so much that one could not see more than a mile ahead, while the banks of the river were covered in dense jungle, reaching down to the water's edge, and the trees were swarmed with long-tailed monkeys and Gibbon apes, the latter making no end of noise as the boats approached.

On Tuesday night we encamped on a flat rock just at the foot of some rapids which marked the Lushai frontier. The whole of the day had been occupied in toiling up swift rapids, and we had gone through many hours of excitement and had not come through free, but had shipped quite a deal of water which had to be bailed out from time to time.

This rock formed a good camping ground, and after cutting down the long grass which grew on the rock, to save being swarmed with leeches, we prepared our evening meal and spread it out on a small camp table, we ourselves sitting on whatever was most convenient. Here I had the pleasure of seeing a very large spider carrying its young ones upon its back, the number of which must have counted to hundreds. One of the natives, however, who was

A dug-out with Mrs. Reginald A. Lorrain, daughter, and Lakher boy in the foreground (*p.* 39).

The Hut in which the Author and his wife with their dog "Crusoe" spent the first two-and-a-half months in Lakher-land (*p.* 70).

[*To face p.* 42.

standing by, on seeing it immediately killed it, and so I was deprived of a good specimen.

From Barkal onward we had had to have four boats instead of three, as they were smaller, and these were moored alongside the rock. Our camp fires were brightly burning and a frugal meal was spread, the kettle boiling and the tea made, and after refreshing the inner man, with a reading from the Word of God and with a quiet prayer we turned in our several boats for the night, the boatmen also turning in at the same time.

During the first part of that night somehow I was unable to sleep, and lay awake for some time listening to the various sounds in the jungle close at hand, which I knew well was infested with tigers. At last I felt that I was unable to stand the cramped position of the boat any longer, and without disturbing my wife who was lying fast asleep by my side, I quietly crawled out, and throwing off the matted covering which shut up the middle opening of the boat I peered out into the bright moonlight, when to my utter surprise I saw some long black object almost in mid-stream, and it took me some few minutes to collect my thoughts before I realised that one of our boats had disappeared.

On a second glance I soon saw that it was the boat containing my brother and his wife that was floating aimlessly down-stream and getting towards the whirling waters of the rapids. She had slipped her moorings and there was no time to lose.

Placing my hands to my mouth I called out as loud as ever I could to my brother who was lying deep in slumber inside the drifting boat, and after a number of calls I managed to wake him up he, peering out from his little burrow, wanted to know what

I was making all the noise about. When I called and told him what was the matter he was indeed thankful that he had heard my call, and waking the Margie and his men, they were enabled after some difficulty to moor the boat securely alongside the other boats again.

It is a wonderful thing how God cares for His children, and how seeming inconveniences often work out to our Salvation; for to lie restless at night is not a pleasing thing, but to lie restless at night in order that another may be saved from a great calamity is indeed a God-send; and had not the drifting boat been seen it would have drifted away down the river mile after mile, and when it arrived at the rapids lower down, it would in all probability have been dashed to pieces and lives might have been lost. How thankful we were to our loving Heavenly Father for His tender care over us in preventing this calamity.

Early the next morning we were off once more up stream, and our boatmen had tedious work in tugging and dragging the dug-outs up the various rapids between the rocks, rowing and poleing being out of the question, the water being extremely shallow. Everything, however, went well with us, and we passed by a little bungalow on the side of the river which proved to be a Government building of the Forest Customs for the Lushai country, where native police were stationed to examine any timber or merchandise that was brought or floated down the river from up country and to levy the Government taxes on the same if any, such as ivory, bamboos, large timber and dug-outs made up country; all were due for taxation. This spot seemed an extremely lonely station and plenty of fever abounded, but after a few minutes' chat with the *Babu* in charge, we made our way up river once again towards our journey's end.

An hour or so had passed by, dense jungle on every hand, and save from the cry of parrots and monkeys, only the sounds that came from our own boats could be heard, when suddenly straight ahead of us on the bank of the river at one of its bends we spied a Jungle Wolf seizing a Barking Deer at the water's edge. The rowers immediately plying their oars with all their strength, made all speed towards the spot, and the wolf with great pluck and determination, tried no less than three times to drag the now dead deer up the steep bank from the river's edge into the jungle beyond.

Seeing us coming it would tug with all its strength, then run up the bank, and thinking it had another opportunity would rush down again, seizing the deer and tried its utmost at removing its heavy prey. Our boatmen, however, proved the better, and when our boats were within about twenty yards of the shore the wolf left its prey and made into the jungle, our boat almost immediately running on to the beach. One of my men and myself jumped out of the boat, and he taking the hind legs while I took the fore, we hoisted the freshly-killed deer into the dug-out and went on our way. Probably the jungle wolf had not very friendly feelings towards us, seeing we had robbed it of its breakfast.

Pulling up stream again we hitched all our boats side by side, and partook of our morning meal, passing the food from one dug-out to the other while the boatmen still plied their oars and poles, thus saving as much time as possible, while the cries of the Gibbon apes were on every hand, and the experience was indeed a pleasant one to those of an adventurous mind.

Towards noon the clouds started to gather and a storm was threatening, which caused us to prepare with all speed to meet the worst.

We soon found we had to tie up under an overhanging tree, lashing our dug-outs as securely as possible, placing the mat covering over three of the boats in such a way as to leave the opening in between available for a chat with one another, and during this heavy storm we partook of our lunch while the rain pelted down with all its power on to our frail bamboo roofs, but we were very thankful that there was not a great amount of wind with this storm as often is the case. Had there been, in all probability the frail bamboo roofs of our boats would have been carried away and we ourselves would have been exposed to the full force of the elements.

The storm lasted a full hour, and just as quickly as the storm had sprung up the sky cleared once again, and the sun beat down upon us with all its brilliance. Very soon everything that had been soaked was perfectly dry once more, and we were able to throw off our mat coverings and let a little fresh air into our tiny quarters.

That afternoon, just before the sun disappeared over the hill tops, with great difficulty we ascended by means of poles and ropes the last rapids ere we arrived at the end of our river journey, at a little place called "Demagiri," the highest point to which we were able to use the dug-outs.

Nothing but a small patch of stones with a high cliff presented itself to our vision, save that high up on the top of this cliff could be seen the roof of a

Government Dâk Bungalow. We therefore ran our boats into a quiet cove, and tying them securely to the bank, the men started to unload, climbing up the steep hillside placed the various boxes on the verandah of the dâk bungalow, where we intended to stay while procuring Lushai natives to carry our loads across the hills, which was to be the next stage of our journey.

The boatmen set to work and skinned the deer which we had secured in the morning, and after it was all prepared the men asked us to kindly accept a leg of it, which we did with many thanks, as it made a pleasant change from the proverbial chicken, and replenished our larder.

CHAPTER V

ACROSS THE HILLS

DEMAGIRI is a little native bazaar where a number of Bengali traders do business with the hills people, and the Government have built a native hospital where they have a Bengali in attendance. During our stay at Demagiri, hour by hour native Lushai Christians from my brother's station arrived to welcome us and to carry our loads back over the mountains to Lungleh, a distance of four days' journey, where my brother and his colleague had worked for many years. Each load had to be arranged so as not to weigh more than between fifty and sixty pounds apiece, and this arranging of loads was a tedious and long task.

Our first impressions of the Lushai tribesmen were various. They struck us as greatly resembling the Mongolian people, but both men and women wore their hair in the same way, namely, tied in a knob at the nape of the neck, and both sexes being dressed in similar fashion the stranger would find it practically impossible to separate the men from the women. However, after being in the country for a little time, the most simple way of distinguishing the sexes is the following.

The men smoke a pipe with a straight stem similar in style to the English pipe, while the women smoke a pipe having a water vessel underneath through which the smoke must pass. Another peculiarity is that the Lushai women wear a large round disc of ivory inserted in the lobe of their ears, whilst the men wear only a small ear-ring. Of course, when a person has been in the country for some time, one soon learns to distinguish the sexes without any trouble.

The Government Dâk Bungalow is worth a moment's consideration. It is a very comfortable bamboo building built upon piles with sawn wood floor, bamboo walls and a galvanized iron roof, having a verandah along the front and at the back. The bungalow is divided into three fair-sized rooms, the centre room acting as a dining-room with a bedroom and a small bath-room leading out of the bedroom on either side, and each room entered by a door opening on to the verandah and in some cases into the dining-room as well. Wooden steps lead from the ground up to the verandah, and the bungalow is furnished with a bed and table, a cupboard and chairs for the dining-room, while the cupboard contains all the necessary crockery, basins, jugs, etc., for a few days' camp. Each bungalow has a caretaker called a Chokedar, and he is supposed to supply the weary traveller with milk, and on this condition does he keep his position, but ofttimes the supply of mik is very scarce. Over the table in the dining-room and sometimes in the bedroom is a punkah, which is very seldom used, travellers preferring to endure the heat rather than having the flapping of the fan so near one's head.

In order to keep the mosquitos in anything like bearable numbers, we were obliged to light a smudge in a bucket and stand it just on the threshold, so that the smoke passed across the doorway.

The bath-room in India simply consists of a small

room with a perforated floor, a large vessel of water standing in one corner. You stand in this room and by the aid of a large tin pour the water over you from head to foot and rub yourself down. One never gets into a bath as one does in the old country, and these shower-baths are very cooling after a hard day's march.

Our loads being completed, the time having come for us to start our journey over the hills, our carriers having all arrived, we started to muster our men, and giving them each their load started them off, ourselves following in their wake.

These natives carry their loads on their backs supported only by a cane wicker-work strap which is placed across their forehead, at the end of which ropes are attached. These ropes fall over the shoulder, down the side of the pack and are tied at convenient length, the loop on one side passing under one of the lower corners and over the opposite lower corner of the load or box, thus making a perfect cradle for the package, the whole weight being borne on the forehead, while the load rests on the back.

From Demagiri to Lungleh we had four days' journey, to traverse a distance of only forty-one miles, the sun beaming down on us with all its power. Up hill, down hill, mile after mile, steadily we rode on, sea ed on our little mountain ponies, along paths that were only a few feet broad, where on the one side was a high wall of jungle and rock, on the other a steep precipice or the exceedingly s eep slope of a hill side which was also covered densely with jungle, consisting of amboos, trees which are evergreen, palms of various species all intertwined with numerous vines. At noon on the first day we halted at a little clearing in the forest, and here we overtook our carriers, who were partaking of their frugal meal of rice and pig flesh, and in some cases of rice and dog flesh, for these people are great lovers of the flesh of the dog. Soon a fire was lighted and the kettle singing on the top of three green bamboos used as a support to hold it over the fire, and after the cravings of the inner man were satisfied, we ourselves, having had a cup of tea, and our ponies having had a snack of bamboo leaves out of the jungle, and a drink of water from the neighbouring spring, pressed onward on our way.

On the first night we arrived at "Tuichong," where another Government rest-house awaited us, and here we found a steel suspension bridge spanning the river which ran close at hand, the only suspension bridge in the whole of the country.

Fruits of various kinds awaited us at this bungalow; a large tray of vegetables was laid out before us containing egg fruit and various other vegetable niceties, while in the fruit line Pawpaws and Bananas were the uppermost, and save for the continual annoyance of the many mosquitos which, in spite of all our care, managed to get inside our mosquito nets, we had a refreshing sleep, and at sunrise started off on our journey again, mounting up the hills higher and higher and then coming down steep places where it was far more desirable to get off our ponies and trust to our own powers than to keep to our saddles with the prospect of probably being hurled down some huge precipice.

Zig-zagging up this mountain, zig-zagging down the other side of it into the valley, crossing numerous streams and rocky places, travelling along the very edge of precipices was the order of the day. During this day's march we passed through the first Lushai Village we had seen. It was a new one, and at its entrance stood a large bamboo gate with hideous emblems representing men, hung up on the side posts. These we learned were placed there to frighten the evil-spirits of sickness away from the village, whilst the village itself was surrounded by a bamboo fence. The village had only recently moved to this spot, for on the site of the old village about a mile away an epidemic had appeared, and from two to four persons in each house had died during the last few months, sweeping off a greater part of the inhabitants, and since their removal to this spot only three of the villagers had passed away.

Passing along another mile of the road we came to the deserted village, which appeared to be quite a large one; and oh! it was a pitiful sight to see those huts standing vacant, and outside of every door were several graves, where many a father, many a mother, many a son or daughter had only recently been placed one after the other.

On these graves were arranged the skulls of animals that the deceased had killed during his hunting days, and there on a stick hung his hunting bag, his pellet bow and numerous other articles which he had used during life. These people had passed away without accepting the Lord Jesus Christ, probably without ever having had the opportunity of knowing of Him, certainly to no great extent. Such a sight brought home before our eyes the terrible responsibility that lay upon us—yes, and upon every reader of these words in every tribe and nation, for every individual, whether in the stress of city life, or in the wild jungles of

Further India, should have the Gospel, for they are all souls for whom Christ died; and if my readers could but have stood with me in that city of the dead, many I am sure would have consecrated themselves and their lives, their money, and their all, to the salvation of souls. But we could not linger here; we were bound on a journey to give to a darkened tribe, the Lakhers, the Gospel, and we passed on and arrived by nightfall at "Lungshen."

The next day being Sunday we remained at Lungshen bungalow, but in the morning my brother and myself retraced our steps to this new village, some three miles distant, and there in the midst of the village street we held a service, I myself only being able at that time, to listen, to stand as a silent witness, while my brother told them of the Love of Christ, of His dying Love to save them. The people did not gather round. If I remember rightly there were two or three children only, sitting close beside us, the girls were at their weaving on the verandahs, or spinning cotton, the old women were drying tobacco leaves in the sun, or combing out the cotton, but they halted in their work to listen to us. Others passed carrying baskets of bamboo water-pots. Others had loads of wood, and as they passed by they would turn and stop to listen, and who can say but that the Word which they heard would spring up in their hearts unto Everlasting Life. After this little service in the heat of the tropical sun we returned to our wives tired out.

In the evening we called all our carriers together, and on the verandah of the dâk bungalow we held an evening service. Amongst these carriers were about twenty-five of my brother's Christian natives and although my wife and myself could not understand a word of the language, yet we noticed that as one after the other prayed the name "Lakher" was uppermost in their prayers. On inquiring of my brother what was the chief thought in their prayers he informed me that they were praying for the Lakhers and our future work amongst them.

How earnestly they seemed to pray and how anxious they seemed to be about the future of these wild peoples! and the thought crossed our minds, "Were the people in the Homeland praying as earnestly as they were praying, and were they as anxious as they were anxious about the Salvation of their southern brethren, whom only a few years before were their bitterest enemies?"

It was a wonderful sight to us: a band of wild head-hunters and devil-appeasers sitting at the feet of Him Who came to save them through the sacrifice of His Own Self—a reward for the lonely Missionaries who had laboured so faithfully amongst those peoples, counting privation and hardship as nought in the years gone by, and a joy unspeakable to think that one day, gathered with those dark-skinned brothers snatched as it were from the burning, in a song of unspeakable joy they shall stand before His Throne and glorify the Lamb that sits upon the Throne in Glory for evermore.

On Monday morning at a very early hour, having partaken of a little refreshment, we pursued our way on throughout the whole of the day, the country being similar to that through which we had passed during the last two days, and arrived ultimately at "Pachang," where we halted for the night. Another dâk bungalow was here, and added once more to our comfort.

We were greeted, however, with the news that a

Government coolie, a Santal, had died during the night in an adjoining hut, not fifty yards from the rest-house. He was taken suddenly ill while on the road between Lungleh and this camp and had to be carried the last part of the journey. A few hours after his arrival he passed away, and it was thought that Cholera was no doubt the cause of his death.

Not wishing our carriers to sleep in the same abode as this man had died in, in case of infection, they came up to our bungalow and slept in the dining-room. They spread their sleeping-cloths on the board floor, the men lying in a row on the one side of the room, while the women slept on the other side of the room feet to feet. As they lay in this position one of the men rose and with bowed head he offered up an evening prayer of thankfulness for the past day's mercies and asked that they might be watched over during the night. Then the light went out and all were soon fast asleep, and we ourselves turned in, thankful for such a comfortable night's lodging.

Morning broke, and we started on the last day's march of this stage of the journey. The road was similar to that which we had traversed all along, but it became a good deal steeper, and as we were anxious to arrive as soon as possible we took a short cut which saved us two miles; but, like all short cuts, they are not the easiest, and this one was no exception to the rule. My poor pony went down on his knees at the start, and we picked our way up the side of this steep hill with great difficulty. Then passing through a mass of bamboo jungle we had to lie nearly flat on our ponies' backs in order to avoid getting entangled with the broken canes and vines. Added to our sorrows we found a huge tree fallen across this old disused path (for such this short cut was), no doubt having been uprooted in one of the many fierce storms that swept these mountain ranges.

Obliged to dismount, it was with great difficulty we managed to get our ponies over at all, and the pony which I was riding was very clumsy and nearly managed to throw himself down the precipice in his clumsy endeavour to cross this huge log. We, however, at last managed to get to the other side without hurt, and when we arrived once more at the main road we were within a mile of Fort Lungleh. Several Bengali Babus, who were stationed there for Government purposes, met us at the top of the hill, and as we passed through the little Lushai village a number of natives were waiting in line to shake hands and welcome us into their midst.

Passing up the steep hill round the edge of a precipice, we entered into Fort Lungleh, where we met a great number more of Lushai Christians. A European lady and their daughter, who were staying there, also met us and invited us in for a cup of tea before completing our journey, which we thankfully accepted.

Fort Lungleh consists of three European bungalows, Government office, dwelling-houses for some 150 Sepoys, and a number of Bengali Babu houses. It also boasts of a Post Office, and is situated seven days' journey from the Lakher country, where we intended to establish a Mission station. This Post Office was to be our nearest touch with the outside world.

Passing through the Fort our ponies picked their way up the mountain side for another two miles, and then suddenly an open spot in the jungle lay before us, while on its highest point the two Mission bungalows of the Baptist Missionary Society stood side by side, the home of my brother and his colleague.

The Christians in the school had erected a triumphal arch, over the top of which was a banner flying with the words in the Lushai language " Hlim takin kan lawm a che u," which translated into English means " We welcome you with great joy." The sides of the arch were decorated with wild plantain stems, and across the top of the arch was printed in English characters " WELCOME." Underneath this in Bengali characters was also the word " Welcome." In this way the Lushai Christians found pleasure in welcoming not only their esteemed Missionaries, but also the future pioneers to the wild Lakher Tribes. What deep-seated love for the extension of the Master's Kingdom must have been in those Christian hearts cannot well be imagined, but it was a sight that could not help but impress us greatly for many days.

Space will not permit me to say much about this part of the country nor the people. Needless to say, we received a hearty welcome, which we much appreciated. As the Rainy Season was drawing near it was impossible for us to go forward into the Lakher Country for a few months, and as my brother's colleague was on his way to England on furlough he kindly placed his bungalow at our disposal for the Rainy Season, where my wife and myself spent a few months in studying the Lushai language before going forward to our life's work.

During this stay many things happened of great interest. Many were our trials and troubles in getting the remainder of our stores up country from below, which we had not been able to bring up the river with us, and I was obliged to take a return journey to Demagiri during this period in order to obtain a number of cases, but just before it was time for us to move forward towards the Lakher Country, we received our last package of goods and chattels.

CHAPTER VI

PIERCING THE UNKNOWN

THE Rainy Season started to die away during the following September, and on the 19th of this month, carriers being procured, we started forth on the last stage of our journey, away into the jungle, away from the white man, away from being in touch with civilization, and with hearts full of prayer and looking forward with expectations towards the great work which lay before us, that through His Grace alone we should be able to accomplish.

My brother and his wife decided to accompany us as far as our field of labour, and with many good-byes to our Lushai friends which we had made during our short sojourn in Lungleh, and after a frugal lunch, my wife and I started on our first day's journey to Zobawk, my brother and his wife following later, deviating from the main road to visit a Lushai village where they decided to spend the evening amongst some of their native Christians.

Well do we remember that day. Slowly picking our way through the dense jungle along the main road that runs between Lungleh and "Haka" (a Government station in the Chin hills of Burma), the sun beaming down on us for several hours, and in one part of the road we had to pass under the ledge of a rock over which the water was rushing in a magnificent fall, hugging the side of the precipice in order to avoid getting drenched.

The sun was setting in the west when the sky suddenly became clouded with heavy storm clouds, and we knew that unless we hurried we should be caught in a rainy season deluge. We hastened on our way, but the carrier with our lunch basket had lagged far behind, and when we were within two miles of Zobawk bungalow down came the rain. The road was steep and our ponies were unable to keep on their feet, so my wife and myself were obliged to get down and lead them. Needless to say, we found it exceedingly hard picking our way down this steep incline, which was more like a river bed than a road, the rain simply flowing along it in a stream. Soaked through to the skin we plodded on our way, and having never been over the road before we had no idea where the bungalow was situated. It became intensely dark, but in the course of about an hour we arrived at cross roads. Taking the one to our left up hill, by way of a change, we found that it led directly to the bungalow.

When we arrived, however, our carriers were missing. The man with the lunch basket was also missing, and it was not until having waited some hour or so that he arrived, but with a lunch basket in rather a precarious condition, he having slipped and sat down on that slippery road and in consequence many of the things were broken.

As soon as our bedding was unstrapped, which is always packed in a ground sheet to save it from getting wet, we divested ourselves of our clothes, wrapping a blanket round us in native fashion, as we had no change. The Chokedar then carried away all our clothes to his smoky kitchen to dry, and after a cup of tea and something to eat we lay down for the night. On the following morning all our clothes were brought to us in a perfectly dry condition and we were able to prepare for the day's march.

On leaving this bungalow we left the last signs of civilization behind us, for to-day we had to branch off to the south along an exceedingly narrow bridle-path which led out to "Sherkor" village.

At the cross-roads we met my brother and his wife, and during each day's journey we had the pleasure of their company, but just before we arrived at the end of the day's march, he and his wife branched off the road to visit one Lushai village after another and to hold meetings amongst the people, whilst we ourselves went on a short distance to put up in a small hut by the wayside.

The travelling throughout the whole of this journey to Sherkor was exceedingly tedious, the road being practically only two feet wide and for the greater part of the way along the very crest of precipices. Every day soon after we arrived in camp it rained, but while on the journey only twice were we caught in a storm, for which we were very thankful.

On the first night we camped at a place known as "Thual-Thu." A mile away from the spot where we camped, high up on the mountain top, was a village of that name, whilst our camping ground was in the depth of the jungle, a small clearing having been made and two small huts erected along with a stable which was barely worthy of the name of *hut*, and that night the "Gayal" (an exceedingly large animal superior in size to the buffalo, also known as "Mitten") belonging to the village serenaded us, tearing at the jungle in their search for food, breaking down the bamboos and bellowing one to the other, and the night being exceedingly dark added to the weirdness of the scene.

When leaving Lungleh we had brought a little Lushai boy along with us who expressed a desire to work for us in Sherkor, and we had also taken his brother-in-law to act as cook on the road. This man had managed to obtain some native beer, of which he had drunk too much during the day's march, and the consequence was that that night he was half stupid. This little lad, whose name was "Lal-sa-vunga," had nightmare, and in the middle of the night he gave such a terrible yell that I jumped out of my camp cot, seized my rifle and ran out thinking that some wild animal had seized him.

I could see nothing, the night was so black, so I made my way over to the little cook hut, there to find the boy lying on his bamboo couch, while his brother-in-law was calmly sitting beside him smoking his pipe and with a grin bluntly informed me that the boy was only dreaming.

There was no rest for us that night, however, and throughout all the years of our travels only one other night of camping in the jungle has been so hideous, and that, was on the anniversary of our wedding day several years later when camping on the banks of the "Kolodyne" river in a hut made of bamboos and leaves, with our pony picketed outside by the camp fire and a tiger on guard at no great distance. All sleep departed from our eyes, and we spent the hours of that lonely night keeping the fires burning and reading the home letters which we had had that day brought to us in the jungle.

We were not sorry when daylight appeared once

again, and the next day's journey to "Minpui" (Village of the Great Landslip) was very similar to the day previous. The hut in which we camped this night was slightly superior to the one in which we had camped the previous night, and as the next day was Sunday we rested, but a very lonely Sunday it was, for in the small confines of this little shanty we had to amuse ourselves, while outside the rain was coming down for many hours, and when at last it passed away the whole ground was so deep in mud that it was impossible to move about. We also were unable to get any healthy drinking water, and the fuel for our fire had run out, so we were obliged to go on very short rations during that day.

Monday morning saw us once more picking our way along the mountain sides towards the next halting place "Chonhu," where our night's abode was no better.

We had now left the Lushai country behind us, and for the next ten miles of the road we were passing through the villages of the Poi people, who had for various reasons been pushed over from the "Chin Hills" in Burma, and had taken up residence in this country. After passing "Longtlai" village, we started the ascent of the "Paitha Range," a long and tedious ascent with a path exceedingly steep and attended with many difficulties, especially for our poor ponies, but from the top of this range we obtained a beautiful view of the whole country, looking right over the main ranges of mountains towards the Burmese frontier, and from this point we came in view for the first time of the great "Kolodyne" river which on the following day we had to cross.

The descent of this range was worse than the

ascent, for the path was very inferior and strewn with many boulders which increased the difficulty of travelling for our ponies, not to mention ourselves, and it was quite impossible for us to keep to the saddle.

On our way down this range of mountains we saw, right across the valley, the long ridge of hills on which "Sherkor" village lay, and in the far distance we could make out the huts of that village which was to be the centre of our labours for the next several years.

That night, after a tedious day's journey, we arrived at the first Lakher village we had ever seen, and this night we had a very superior abode, for a family of Lakhers in a newly-built hut kindly consented to turn out and go into some neighbour's house in order that we might occupy their dwelling.

How our hearts beat within us. At last the dreams of over two years had become a reality. We were actually in the midst of a Lakher village with nothing but the Lakher language being spoken around us, save for one or two who understood a few words of the Lushai language.

There was no likeness between these people and their neighbours the Lushais. They were quite a different nation. Much darker, and their manners and customs were quite different. Their huts, too, were of superior size, and the front walls of these huts were ornamented with lattice work in order that they should be cooler, but the people and many of the huts themselves were certainly a great deal dirtier than their neighbours the Lushais.

That night we held a meeting in the village in the Lushai language, the old chief interpreting for us to the best of his ability, the substance of the meeting being for the greater part the objects of our coming amongst them to be their Missionaries.

I will not pause here to say anything about their manners and customs, as that is dealt with in a later chapter, but we were exceedingly pleased with the general aspect of the people amongst whom we had come to reside, yet we were not at our journey's end, for there was still one day's march before us.

Bidding good-bye to these villagers, using the Lushai language of which very few of them understood anything, we passed through the village into the jungle, and they catching on to the spirit of the salutation bade us "good-bye" in their own tongue with the words "A tla-pa-ta-ta khy mu vy," which is their exceedingly lengthy farewell, and meaning "May you go up in good health."

Descended into the valley, passing over numerous mountain torrents, piercing the dark jungle, at this part of the road consisting mostly of large trees with plenty of undergrowth, we at last came to the banks of the Kolodyne river in the valley, a very wide, deep and rapid river at this time of the year, the heavy rains sweeping down huge trunks of trees and other débris from the upper reaches.

Here the Government had just lately placed a little dug-out with two or three natives as boatmen, and in this little dug-out we had to make our way some long distance up the river, hugging the bank before striking across, but the swiftness of the current was so much that ere we reached the other bank we landed exactly opposite to the place where we had started, and in this manner all our carriers and all our baggage crossed the "Kolodyne." Our ponies then had to be taken a long way up the river, and they were one at a time ferried across, their heads being held above water by the man in the dug-out. We watched anxiously on the bank for their safe arrival, but the current was so exceedingly strong that it was quite impossible to land the ponies at the regular crossing, and they were swept some quarter of a mile further down the river, where a little road had to be cut through the jungle in order that they might be brought up to the mountain path.

Thankful when all this anxiety was over, and God in His Mercy suffered us to see no loss of any of our goods, we followed the Kolodyne river down stream for two and a half miles when we came to a large mountain torrent which was spanned by a native bamboo bridge made simply of a bundle of long bamboos thrown across the river and being secured at either side with cane ties, and tiers of stones encased in a bamboo matted bin being the chief supports, while the sides were in a V-shape, acting as a railing to save one from tumbling into the boiling waters below. It was very much like crossing a tight rope, and here we had great difficulty in getting our ponies across, but ultimately all was safely on the other side, and saddling the ponies once again we started the ascent of the 2,000 feet which was to bring us up on to the mountain ridge where Sherkor village was situated, and where the first Missionary station was soon to be erected.

It was a weary climb after a hard day's march, of which the fording of the Kolodyne river, swimming the ponies across, and getting our many loads of goods and provisions safely over, had proved the most fatiguing, and our ponies climbed the steep ascent very slowly, but ultimately we reached the top of the ridge where the road lay a little more level and even.

Just before four o'clock in the afternoon "Sherkor" village loomed in sight. Our hearts were full of eager expectation at the sight of our new country, and yet no one came out of the village to meet us. At all the other villages as we approached men and children came out to meet us, carrying a bunch of bananas or a sugar cane as a welcome, but here at "Sherkor" no one stirred, and as we entered the village there seemed to be very few people about. In the centre was an exceedingly large hut built on piles, which was the abode of the Chief, whose name was "Thylai."

As we approached his verandah we found him sitting there with his wife, a few children and several adults by him, while two or three other men strolled across to have a look at us. His wife presented my brother's wife and my own with a stick of sugar cane, and after passing a few words of greeting and arranging with the old Chief (for he was somewhere near seventy years of age) to have a Council of War on the verandah in the evening, we proceeded on our way through the village towards some huts at the further end, where we decided to make our camp.

The huts here were indeed a great improvement on those we had been occupying during the last six nights, and the one my wife and myself occupied consisted of two large rooms and a little side room which had to be utilised as a bath-room at one end and a pantry at the other, whilst one room was used for a living-room and the other for a bedroom. It was by no means an elaborate affair, the chief thing about it being that it had a good roof made of bamboo ; but on the other hand one could see the daylight through almost every inch of the walls, and the doors were simply slabs of plaited bamboo which pushed along and had no means of fastening securely. A few days, however, soon made this little abode comfortable, and rummaging over our various loads my wife soon found some curtains, a table-cloth and a carpet with which she made the place cosy as only a wife knows how.

On the first night of our arrival we held the Council of War on the Chief's verandah, which was somewhere about 24 feet square.

A bright wood fire burned in the clay hearth, the smoke curling its way up to the roof and finding exit into the air from the front of the verandah. Two logs of wood cut in the form of an hour-glass were brought out for my brother and myself to sit on, our wives not being present, whilst opposite us squatted the Chief and his wife, and round in a large circle numbers of our Lakher friends, the headmen of the village, were assembled. One young Lakher acted as interpreter, as all our conversation had to be carried on in the Lushai language. We first of all mentioned our reason for coming into the midst of them, and asked if they were pleased at our arrival, pleased that they might have a white man which they might call their own and who had come to help and befriend them in any way possible and to tell them of the Wonderful Love of God and of His Son, Jesus Christ ? The reply to this was in the affirmative, and to our asking the question if the Chief was agreeable to our building somewhere near to the village on a site which should be decided upon during the next few days, he willingly agreed.

That night's meeting remains firm in my mind,

A general view of Sherkor Village looking across the Kolodyne Valley (*p.* 67).

" Thylai," Chief of Sherkor, a great hunter of wild animals and human heads.

The Author in Lakher dress.

[*To face p.* 68.

for it was only the second time it had been my privilege to be amongst a large group of these wild Lakher hillsmen, and the wood fire that flared up sent its sparks up to the roof and lit up the chocolate-coloured faces with their various ornaments in their hair, giving to the whole scene a very livid appearance.

In about two hours' time the Council of War was over, and after bidding them good-night, we wended our way along the dark, steep village street which was little better than the bed of a river, for huge rocks and boulders were everywhere, and one had to go with care.

Our wives were glad to see us back again, and after a frugal meal, and full of thankfulness to God for having brought us at last to our desired haven and permitting us to be His Ambassadors in this strange and wonderful land, and with a word for the Blessing of God to rest on all the loved ones left behind, we turned into our beds for the first time in Sherkor, Lakherland, glad to realize that at last the long and tedious journey was over and that we were actually in the land to which the Lord had called us some two and a half years previous.

CHAPTER VII

ALONE, YET NOT ALONE

FIRST impressions and first experiences in any new epoch of life, when one looks back from years after into the past and perceives how one thing has led on to another in perfect rotation and to the advancement of the cause, are full of interest and inspiration to those who trust in the Lord.

The sun rose, and with it we ourselves entered on to the first day's experience in a new and strange and wonderful land, amongst an unknown people who spoke an unknown tongue, whose manners and customs were unknown to us, and whose very faces were far from familiar and whose skins varied from ours to almost the extent that black differs from white.

We found ourselves bustling round our little bamboo hut, making the little abode which was to be our home for the next two and a half months as comfortable and cosy as it was possible under the circumstances. Our first meal was spread, and thanking God for preserving us during the past night, we sat down to partake of it, while outside of the hut with staring eyes stood a large crowd of Lakher children and Lakher men and women watching us manipulate to their great wonder our knives and our forks, and eating our food seated upon chairs—a thing totally unknown amongst themselves naturally, for squatting on the ground with a common dish of rice in their midst, seizing their food by their hand and thrusting it into their open mouth, was the only manner in which they knew wherewith to supply the inner man with the necessary food.

The meal over, my brother and myself with one or two Lushai natives, and at some distance following in our wake a small line of Lakhers, in Indian file, we entered into the jungle, climbing up the steep side of the mountain, forcing our way through the undergrowth sometimes with ease, other times having literally to cut our way, we scoured the mountain side in order to find a suitable place on which to build our future home. Clearing a part of the jungle here and there of undergrowth, and surveying the surrounding country was no easy matter, but when we thought we had a good position we set to work to clear a larger amount of the jungle, as it was practically impossible to see how suitable it might be for building until much of the undergrowth had been cut away for some distance.

Having brought out a number of plants with us, such as a few banana trees, a few flowering plants, and a few fruit trees with which to start a garden, we selected a spot to plant these for the time being, and in a very small space, very closely together, were they placed with a strong fence surrounding them to protect them from domestic animals and wild animals that might happen to pass that way. The spot, however, which we had cleared for the erection of a building was not suitable, and we were obliged to go lower down the hill side and clear another large space of undergrowth, after which we determined that this was the spot where we should build, being within about a quarter of a mile of the spring where we should have to draw our water and at a sufficiently high elevation to catch the cooler breezes that should blow across the Kolodyne Valley.

Day by day from early morning till late in the afternoon we worked upon this spot, and at last were able to place four bamboos on the site, each one marking a corner of the proposed bungalow.

During these first few days many interesting things happened, and being towards the end of the rainy season, the Lakhers had their fish traps on the rivers built, and several days we were able to purchase a few fish of them which replenished our larder, food being none too abundant with us.

One evening my brother and his wife, my wife and myself took a stroll through Sherkor village, where most of the people were deeply engaged in feasts of all sorts and in drinking bouts. The night was very dark, and after looking upon many of these scenes with wonder and longing that the Lord would use us to lead these people into the Truth which is in Jesus Christ, we wended our way up the steep hill side through the village towards our little hut, which stood alone at some little distance from the extreme end. When we came within about a hundred yards of the hut, my brother and I spied a strange light gleaming through its matted walls. We looked at one another for a second only, then almost with one breath we exclaimed, "The hut's on fire inside!"

Leaving our wives we tore along that path in breathless haste, and flinging open the flimsy door we found the whole partition of the hut in flames, crackling and burning at a furious rate. Seizing whatever was handy we set to work to smother the fire, which mercifully to relate we were soon able to overcome. Had we been but a minute or two later at the most every effort would have been hopeless; our hut would have been burned to the ground; all our goods which were in baskets and boxes inside would have been sacrificed to the flames, and we should have found ourselves in a strange land amongst a strange people, homeless, foodless and penniless, practically with nothing in the world save the clothes that were on our backs.

How thankful we were to our Loving Heavenly Father for having directed our steps homeward at that moment and having allowed our eyes to detect the strange light within those matted walls, thus saving all the terrible privation that might have so easily befallen us at that time in our career.

When we left our hut we had left a little bracket carriage lamp hooked on to the partition, and having no cocoanut oil or colza oil we had filled the vessel with kerosine, our only means of light. Turning it very low, we left, and it appeared that the burner was not suitable for the kerosine. It had become very much heated and had heated the whole of the lamp, melting all the solder with which it was fastened together, and caused the bottom of the lamp to slowly slide, the flame catching the bamboo which was exceedingly dry, and it immediately blazed up, burning the lamp to pieces, melting many of its parts and leaving it utterly useless. Needless to say, we learned a great lesson from this fire, and ever after when leaving a light in a bamboo house, we leave it in the form of a lantern suspended on a long wire from the ceiling, it being impossible to knock it over from the floor, by any animal, and should it explode it would be unable to reach any of the walls.

My brother and his wife had stayed with us for ten days, and the morning had now arrived when we must bid each other good-bye, while they took their journey to the North back again to Fort Lungleh, my wife and myself to be left alone amongst the Wild Hillsmen of Lakher.

We accompanied them along the road for about a mile, passing through the village, along the ridge till we came to a bend in the road. At this spot there stands a very large tree, large in girth, with a tall, straight trunk. Here we decided should be our parting point, this tree to stand ever after in our minds for a remembrance of that lonely parting which the first Pioneers to Lakher had to undergo.

Good-byes were said, my brother and his wife mounted their little mountain ponies, and with many words of cheer from my brother we saw them ride away along the jungle path into the dense jungle beyond, and when out of sight my wife and I turned our faces towards our little hut, walking along the road realizing that we were alone, she and I, with no other white person near, nor likely to be near for some long stretch of time.

Yes, we felt lonely, but lonely though we were, yet we were not alone, for He Who had promised never to leave us was with us to comfort and to bless, but we realized that, humanly speaking, in future we were to be all in all to one another, and according to our unity and love towards one another and towards the Work which we had undertaken in the Name of the Lord, and which He had undertaken to carry out through our instrumentality, so was that Work to prosper and our lonely exiled life to be a life of joy, unity and communion with Him.

Thus far God had opened up our way step by step, one thing leading upon another to the establishment of a Mission amongst these wild people. God had also put it into the hearts of the Goverment officials in the Lushai Hills, on whose extreme boundary we were residing, to help us in many ways over the great difficulties that confronted us, especially in regard to house building, for the Government Official at Lungleh at this time showed great favour towards us, and through his kindness we were enabled to get natives to help with the building of our bungalow, without whose help at that time we hardly know what we should have done, for the Lakhers were not fond of work and almost all their wants being supplied from within, were not at all anxious to be tempted by money, which they hardly knew the sight of, or by articles of merchandise.

God, however, had provided the way for us, and for the next two months and a half, with the aid of these natives, from daylight till dark, we laboured, erecting a suitable abode for the next few years' residence. My wife, attending to the household duties, making and cooking her own bread, utilizing the things at hand to meet our every need, was busy in our humble abode at the foot of the hill, while our dog "Crusoe" kept her company throughout the day during my absence, and every afternoon, to save my leaving the work at tea hour, she would spread the table under the shade of an overhanging tree close to our building operations.

Day by day saw the development of the building work. All our material for house building had to come from the jungle. Small tree trunks constituted the posts to support the walls. Bamboos split open and woven together formed the material for the walls, which being placed double with the shiny outside of the bamboo towards the inside of the house and also towards the outside, the inner parts of the bamboos coming together, made a stout wall. These large matted walls were fastened securely to the posts by means of cane ties. The roof was formed of young saplings, on the top of which were tied whole bamboos covered thickly over with a species of cane leaf, and these leaves being covered over with slats of bamboo fastened securely down with cane.

Thus our bungalow was erected without the use of a single nail, the whole building being fastened securely together by means of cane ties, with an 8-ft. verandah in front and a narrow verandah running round the other three sides.

It was a long and tedious work, and took us practically two months and a half to make it at all fit for habitation, and after we had commenced living in our newly-built bungalow several months had to be spent in making the place a little more homely and in making furniture, all of which had to be made of material brought from the jungle, with the exception of the tables, which we constructed from our packing cases, and it was with a sense of pleasure that we at last looked upon our completed Pioneer Mission Station.

In order, however, to get a small piece of flat land on which to erect our bungalow, we had in the first place to cut off the top of a hill, fill in a little hollow with the earth and rock, and the rest of the earth and rock that was cut away had to be drawn out in front of the level place, making it slightly wider and suitable for a small front garden. When this was completed the front of the bungalow was raised eight feet from the garden in front, whilst the back of the bungalow was level with the ground. The cutting of the earth was probably the most tedious work of the lot, but it had to be done, there being no flat land available in any direction.

During the midst of the building operations the natives who were helping me with the building suddenly set up a cry, uttering words the meaning of which I did not then understand, and springing down from their lofty positions on the roof of the bungalow started in one band to rush down the steep mountain side towards the village, each man grasping his large chopper in his hand. Not knowing the meaning of this I picked up my rifle and ran with them under the impression that they were chasing some wild animal which they had espied.

However, they led me straight into the village, and there on my arrival what should I behold but one of the native huts all in flames. It was a house on fire, and from their lofty position on the roof of our bungalow they were able to see the flames, whereas to myself, standing on the ground, they were invisible. But we were too late. The hut was burned to the ground, but the occupants had saved their few belongings just in time.

Seeing I was carrying my rifle, they asked me why I had brought it, and could not help laughing at me for not having understood what they said.

It was during this house building that I started to get a foundation of the language, there being no books, no written language, nothing to help one. It was extremely difficult, for the language had to be picked up word by word, and each word I noted in my pocket-book over and over again, and during these two months and a half I started to get just a smattering of this strange tongue.

During this time also we had found it extremely hard to procure sufficient food, especially in the way of vegetables and flesh, and several times I had been obliged to take my rifle and go out into the jungle to shoot whatever bird I might see that was good for food, and if a squirrel happened to cross my path that too went into our larder. Our little boy, "Lal-sa-vunga," who had come out with us from the Lushai country, used to attend to the camp fire and see to the cooking of the rice. On the day to which I refer my wife had dealt out to him the last of our scanty supply of rice, which we were going to have with a tin of salmon for our lunch. Falling to sleep, he allowed the whole saucepan of rice to burn to a cinder. Thus we had nothing but a tin of salmon to eat, and something having happened to our yeast which was made of bananas, we were unable for a few days to obtain bread. Going from hut to hut in the village I endeavoured to persuade the people to sell me a cucumber to eat with our salmon, and after about an hour's wandering from house to house I managed to procure two, and with these treasures I hastened back to my wife, who welcomed them for our noonday lunch. After this little incident, our supply of tinned meat having run out, I was obliged to shoot our dinner, and when unsuccessful we had to go without meat. The only time available for hunting was in the very early hours of the morning, and ofttimes between three and four I had to bestir myself in order to get a shot at a wood pigeon or the like.

Being so far removed from civilization, stores were not procurable at a moment's notice, and being inexperienced at that time we continually found ourselves running out of this and that necessity. Sugar and tea were things that for very many months we had to go without, but after our first year in this lonely land of many hard experiences, we learned the art of keeping ourselves supplied with the necessities of life.

One evening as we sat, at the close of a hard day's work, by the door of the hut, before we had entered into our new home, a band of Lakhers carrying a huge land tortoise (about 18 inches by 24 inches in diameter) appeared, and asked us to purchase the same, which we eagerly did as our larder was very low. It was alive, and having read in books of adventures in days gone by of how shipwrecked people had captured tortoises on the seashore and turning them on their backs to save them escaping into the sea and leaving them in this topsy-turvy position until they were needed for food, we decided to place this huge land tortoise in the corner of our living room turned on its back for the night, and for several hours before we retired to bed it remained in this position complacently.

Bed-time came and we retired, shutting the bamboo-woven door which separated the bedroom from the living room, with our friend the tortoise still lying on its back. That night round our hut a herd of domestic Gayal from the village serenaded us, browsing on the various weeds and pulling at the undergrowth, snorting and bellowing and disturbing the quietness of the night, whilst in the distance from several points of the compass we could hear the barking of barking deer as they wandered through the jungle in the darkness. However, we were getting used to these sounds, and they did not disturb us so much as they had done at the commencement, and my wife and myself were soon in dreamland, when all of a sudden,with a start, we both awoke with a noise of what apparently appeared to us the opening of the door of our hut which we had fastened by means of a bamboo and cane on the inside for the night.

The noise of the Gayal, the weird sounds of the jungle, the grating and giving way of the bamboo matting in our half-slumbering condition immediately aroused suspicions in our mind that something unusual was happening, and our first thoughts turned naturally to some hostile intention of the tribe amongst whom we resided. Springing out of our bed we soon had a lantern alight, and very cautiously we drew back the door which separated the bedroom from the living room, to see if by chance we might ascertain the cause of the disturbance, when to our great surprise we found that our friend the tortoise had gone and the door of our hut was securely fastened.

A short search of the living room soon showed us our friend wedging himself between the partition of our bedroom and one of the bamboo posts which supported it, and so strong was he that he was forcing the two apart. This accounted for the noise we had heard together with the sounds of the Gayal and the jungle.

Eased in our minds, and surprised to find that the tortoise had managed to right himself and to get away from his position of lying on his back, we took a large rope and tied it securely in two strands round his shell, the other end of which we tied tightly to one of the supports of the wall of the hut. Satisfied that now he would not be able to go beyond his tether, we returned to our bed, rejoicing that nothing worse had happened, and soon were fast asleep.

How long we slept I know not, but we were awakened very suddenly by a terrible crash of china close at hand. Springing up once again we entered our living-room and there to our surprise we found our friend the tortoise had escaped from his lashings and had found his way to the further side of the hut, where there was erected in the corner a bamboo table containing several shelves on which we had placed the greater part of our crockery. He had wedged himself between the wall and the supports of this bamboo table, which was simply tied together with cane, and with his mighty strength had forced the supports apart, the shelves immediately giving way and letting the whole of the crockery fall down upon him, much of which we found smashed to small fragments all over the floor.

We were at our wits' end what to do with this tortoise. He had indeed become a costly customer situated as we were, beside all the terrible forebodings that he had brought up in our minds during the night, and he had now deprived us of many valuable utensils that could not be replaced speedily. Our first intention was to open the hut door and politely place him outside and allow him to find his way into the jungle and to liberty, but food in our larder being very low we were very reluctant in doing this, and in night attire, in that dark room with the flicker of an oil-burning lantern, we talked over the situation.

At last we determined to see if we could not fasten this tortoise so that he should not do any more damage or give us any further trouble until daylight, so cutting two pieces of bamboo about eighteen inches long, we placed one of these between the top and lower shell where his head and his feet protruded, and the other piece between the top and the lower shell at the tail end, which fitted into the grooves very nicely. Taking our big rope we tied these two bamboos securely at both ends, and then as an extra precaution we turned him on his back, lashing his shell to the support of the wall of the hut.

It was now impossible for him to either put out his head or his feet, and leaving him thus we turned into bed once again to endeavour to get an hour or two's sleep ere morning should bring another day's labours. This time we had overcome all difficulties. He proved himself unable to get away, and the rest of that night was spent in peace.

The next morning we got some Lakhers to kill it and to take off its shell, so that we might cook the flesh and eat it, and which supplied us with meat for quite a number of days. It was delicious eating, but the flesh of the animal after it had been killed continued to move for quite a number of hours and we both declared that delicious as it was we should never again care to eat an animal so tenacious to life as this tortoise proved to be.

The incident which I mentioned towards the beginning of this book of how the Lakhers had crossed the frontier, seized a family of slaves and carried them back, stringing the father of the family up to a tree, with the result that the British Government determined to send an expedition, and thus a road that was to lead us out to Sherkor was cut, so now at this time as Christmas was fast approaching, the expedition was at last upon its way to punish those Lakhers for their accumulated offences, and during the middle of December numbers of mules laden with ammunition and all necessaries for the expedition, passed along the narrow mountain path past our bungalow, whilst these were followed by numerous companies of Sepoys, each with his full war equipment ready should the Lakhers determine to resist the expedition.

This of course was quite an exciting time, and the Lakhers themselves had never seen so many Sepoy soldiers armed and prepared for battle, whilst numerous mules bearing small cannons on their backs followed these regiments, while a long line of native carriers, nearly all of which were of the Lushai tribes, followed up the rear laden with provisions for the troops; and after these had all passed on seven miles beyond our bungalow to the camping ground before their approach to Zongling, the offending village, the European Officers in charge with a military doctor arrived, namely, Lieut.-Col. Cole, Lieut.-Col. Loch and Mr. Hurst, the latter being the medical officer. These three gentlemen visited our bungalow and were enabled to glance round our new Mission station in the short time at their disposal before passing on, and they very kindly congratulated us on the great amount of work which we had been enabled to accomplish during our two and a half months' residence. After a light lunch we bade them good-bye, and they followed on to join the regiment of Sepoys at the camping ground seven miles further on.

I had been invited to go out to them on the following day to have a cup of tea before they proceeded to Zongling, so early in the afternoon on the following day I bade my wife good-bye for a few hours, and taking two native boys with me I started out on foot to reach their camping ground at "Tuipang" by tea-time.

It was a hard seven miles' walk over a very rough mountain path, and in some cases exceedingly steep, which made it all the more fatiguing, but the scenery through the jungle was magnificent.

We arrived there in safety, and had the pleasure of seeing the whole of the expedition party gathered together and preparing for their advance on the following morning. After shaking hands and expressing a hope that the expedition would be carried out without bloodshed and yet with satisfaction, my two Lakher lads and myself turned our faces towards home, Lieutenant-Colonel Loch kindly insisting on my riding his pony for part of the way at least and sending along with it his *syce* (groom), for which I was very thankful.

Night was fast drawing on and daylight was fast disappearing, so jumping from the saddle I handed the pony over to the *syce* and sent him back with another word of thanks to the Colonel, while leading the way, my two native boys following, and carrying in our hands a torch made of bamboo which we had ignited by means of a fire which we made on the path, we trudged on mile after mile along the brink of those huge precipices through the dense jungle infested with numerous wild animals, and very late that night we arrived safely at the bungalow once again after an exciting and dangerous journey.

How often in my boyhood days when reading books of adventure and travel in various parts of the world my soul had gone out in longing for similar experiences, and here I found myself in the midst of a wild head-hunting tribe of savages, traversing through dense jungles in the dense darkness of an Indian night with a rifle under my arm and a large bamboo torch in my hand, while two native lads, sons of head-hunters, were following in the rear. Since that night many journeys have we taken through the dense jungle by torchlight along the crest of huge and dangerous precipices, hearing on every hand the cries of numerous wild animals, and many times have we heard the cry of the King of these Jungles, the tiger, close at hand, and yet God in all His Mercy has protected us, kept us, guided us, held us, and brought us safely through, and surely we, His servants, who have been commissioned to take these dangerous journeys for His Glory and Honour, that dark-skinned savages for whom He shed His Life's Blood on Calvary's Tree might hear His voice and, hearing, bow before His Throne in repentance, and repenting might live again and be redeemed by His Precious Blood, should trust Him wholly and show our faith in His ever-comforting and emphatic promise—"Lo, I am with you alway, even unto the end"—and does not the Loving Master Who has blessed His creatures so abundantly expect of all that own His name in the Homeland, that they should uphold His Ambassadors in the thick of the fight, exposed as they are to trial, temptation, perils by water, perils by sea, perils by land, perils by fire, perils by storm and in peril of man and beast and ofttimes in peril of death, by their prayers and their consecrated purses, that His Will may be fulfilled and that His servants in the far-off foreign field or wherever they may be, should not lack.

Christmas came, our first Christmas in Lakherland, and naturally our minds turned towards the Homeland, to all our loved ones, and we spent an extremely lonely Christmas, sickness abounding throughout the village and our medicine and medical aid was much desired. On Christmas Day we rested, and during the afternoon my wife and myself endeavoured to banish our loneliness in various hymns, for it was a lonely Christmas, the loneliest one we have ever spent. We had news from the expedition from time to time; Lieut.-Col. Cole kindly sending several messages to tell us how things were progressing and how he had been received by the Lakhers amicably, and how everything had gone smoothly with the expedition and the people made to pay their twenty guns as a punishment without bloodshed, and ended by wishing us as happy and as peaceable an existence in Lakherland for the spread of the Gospel of Jesus Christ as they had experienced during this expedition. These warm messages, coming as they did to us at this time, were very comforting, and throughout all our life we shall never forget them. They seemed to us to have been God-sent messages of cheer.

On the last day of the year the expedition returned, having completed its work, and we had another very pleasant meeting with our own countrymen once more; and I would like to mention here the kindness with which we were treated by these gentlemen, for they were extremely kind to us and towards our work for the Lord, taking an immense amount of interest in our New Pioneer Station and in our exceedingly hard position as pioneers, endeavouring from time to time as far as their power lay to help us in many ways in regard to obtaining native carriers for our loads of provisions from over the mountains, and also enabling us to obtain fowls from

The Pioneer Mission Bungalow, Sherkor, Lakher-land (*p.* 76).

"Crusoe," the faithful companion of the first years of pioneering (*p.* 87).

[*To face p.* 86.

various villages regularly, we ourselves being absolutely unable to procure any at that time, and allowing us the use of the Government *dâk* runners for carrying our mails, keeping us in communication with the outside world almost regularly twice a month.

These little kindnesses rendered towards us ofttimes saved us much privation, which, had not the Lord raised them up to help us in these matters, we should have been called upon to undergo.

One of our greatest comforts at this the start of our pioneering in Lakherland to both my wife and myself was our good dog "Crusoe," who was exceedingly faithful and became as one of the family; and when I was absent from the bungalow he would never condescend to leave my wife's side, but would sit faithfully with her, and on hearing my footsteps returning, would meet me on my entering the front garden gate with many a bark and a bound.

Crusoe, however, after pioneering the first year and a half with us, jumped up on his chair to sleep one night by the side of our bed. He had not been asleep more than about half an hour when he awoke with a sharp bark and immediately fell to the floor dead.

We felt as if one of the family had left us, and Sherkor became still more lonely.

CHAPTER VIII

RELIGIOUS BELIEFS

BEFORE introducing our reader to the home life, manners and customs of these interesting people, a few words of explanation in reference to their name will at this time be of interest.

We have introduced them as the Lakhers, but this name is not the correct name for the people, and is both foreign in pronunciation and spelling to the whole language. Their true name, and the name which they call themselves, is " Mara," but by the surrounding tribes they are known as the "Lakhers," and under this name Government has learned to know them and the name has come into such frequent use that it is most unlikely that the civilized world will ever know them by any other.

The Mission also was founded under that name, we at that time being ignorant of the fact that it was not their true name, but in a book of this character it is quite necessary that the reader should be informed on this matter, and as the surrounding tribes and the Government have so firmly fixed this name upon the people it is expedient that they should be known to us under the word " Lakher."

The Lakhers consist of a number of tribes, having a dialect slightly differing one from the other, but the chief tribe of all the tribes of Lakhers boasts of the name of " Tlôsai," and it was quite necessary that the language should be reduced in the dialect appertaining to the chief tribes in the country; and from our study of the language we found that any one acquiring a thorough knowledge of the "Tlôsai Dialect" is able to communicate with all other tribes of Lakhers throughout the whole country with understandable ease, and in the course of a few years as the knowledge of reading and writing increases throughout the country the whole of the various dialects will undoubtedly be swallowed up by the Tlôsai Dialect in the rising generation, and thus the Scriptures and other books translated in this dialect will reach every Lakher throughout the length and breadth of the country.

The Lakher tribes are a self-contained people, having few wants that cannot be supplied from within. On our first reaching the country we found that the King's *Rupee* and the *eight anna piece* were practically the only coins that were known, and then these were known only by a select few who had managed in one way and another to obtain them, boring a hole through the top and hanging them round their necks as an ornament. The smaller coins were practically unknown, but they soon took a fancy to the *pice piece* for an ornament, and one of the great difficulties with us was that they did not require the money and therefore would not part with any vegetables or rice. We, however, had to teach them the value, but we soon found that to start with we were bound to substitute the money for something else if we were to manage to live and procure any native products, so were obliged to buy large quantities of salt and ship it out to our very remote station and use it for barter from day to day. In this way we were able to procure vegetables and rice, and now and again some other variety of food in exchange for the salt.

One case in particular comes up before my mind, where a Lakher woman was passing with a basket of vegetables on her back, the basket being supported by the proverbial rope and mat-strap support across the forehead. My wife wishing to purchase some egg fruit from her, offered her a *two anna piece*, equal to twopence, for them, but there was nothing that would please her save my wife giving to her *four pice*, which is equal to four farthings, in order that she might hang them round her neck as an ornament. We tried to explain to her that *two annas* were twice four farthings, but she sincerely believed that we were trying to rob her, and ultimately she went off very satisfied with her *four pice*, half the amount she had at first been offered.

Now, however, they have for the most part learned better, for we made it our business to teach every one of them who should visit our bungalow the difference in the coins and their equivalents, with the result that now one very seldom meets with a Lakher who does not know the value of coins; and through knowing the value the want of money is gradually encroaching upon them, which is a sure sign of advance, for as long as they do not require money it is almost impossible to obtain labour or help of any kind, and thus the people would remain in a far more unconcerned condition as regards their place in helping forward the progress of the world and in learning that there is glory and honour in honest work and not shame.

The manners and customs of the Lakhers and their folklore are all of great interest, but a great part of their folklore is such that it is difficult to place it in English terms without committing one's self to great vulgarity, while on the other hand these same things which would appeal to the highly civilized mind of the Englishman as vulgar and inexpedient, would in the primitive minds of the Lakhers be without spot or blemish, and in the following matter I will endeavour to place before my readers as truly as lies in my power the actual manners and customs of those deeply interesting people.

In the first place there is a most emphatic belief in God, the Giver and Preserver of life, Who is known to them as "Khazopa"; but they do not know God as the Only True God, believing that every man, woman and child has his or her own special god to look after and protect them, and if any harm comes to any person they will immediately say "His god is bad"; and yet while believing that every person has their own special god there is an underlying belief that instead of there being a number of gods there is probably only One, for they most emphatically show forth this belief in their practice of offering the sacrifice of a large pig to God at certain periods of their life, sometimes once in five years and sometimes more often, and at these times a whole family will meet together in their hut and offer up the sacrifice of one pig only to their God, believing that through this sacrifice health and happiness shall rest upon their home.

Besides this God, the Giver and Preserver of life, there are names for four other gods, but any knowledge in reference to them is almost obsolete, while all these names probably refer to the same god or gods, and their business is to look after "Khazopa," the Giver and Preserver of life, and they have nothing whatever to do with human beings.

The Lakhers most emphatically believe in a future state of existence, and the abode of the dead is called "A Thi-pa Khi," namely, "The Dead Man's Village," the abode of all those that die a natural death; while the future state of all those that die an unnatural death, namely, having been slain in battle, killed by tigers or wild animals or through accident, would be in the "Saw Vaw Khi," the village of the victims of misadventure.

The Lakhers most emphatically believe in a Heaven of joy, in contradistinction to the dead man's village, and which is probably best termed "Paradise," but in order to reach this haven of bliss at death it was considered necessary for a man to obtain through hunting, one head of each of the larger animals, such as the tiger, the elephant, the Samber deer, the bear, and many others; and also the head of at least one human being. It was partly on account of this belief that the Lakhers were so keen on head-hunting and that so many tales of massacre, slaughter and bloodshed have been told in years that have passed, and which if only they could be recorded in cold type would probably make some of the most stirring tales that have ever been written.

How these wild hillsmen risked their lives in order to obtain heads of human beings and of these wild animals is marvellous, ofttimes piercing the dense jungle in their hunting expeditions day after day, week after week, until their food supply had been entirely exhausted, existing simply on whatever food they might find in the dense jungle, suffering great privation, this being done for the greater part with the one object of being considered great amongst their own people, and in endeavouring to obtain in their future state greater reward.

All these trophies of the hunt were brought to their village, and over each head, either those of beasts or of human beings, had to be performed the ceremony which is known as "Ia": that is, the warrior had to take from his own domestic animals one head of stock, either a pig or a gayal, and sacrifice it amidst many rites and ceremonies on behalf of this head, believing that by the death of this domestic animal he would obtain power in the future state over the spirit of this animal or human being which he had been fortunate enough to overcome. Thus in the case of human beings each one that fell under his hand would in the future life become his slave.

The "Ia" ceremony would last from three to five days, the flesh of the sacrifice being eaten by all those invited to the feast, while large quantities of rice beer would be drunk by all, and day and night the ceremony would be kept up, whilst all the trophies of the hunt belonging to the warrior would be brought out in full splendour, and girls and young men would dance their most peculiar dances until the whole party were lying practically prostrate with exhaustion and intoxication.

The honour conferred upon a man for having killed a human being was that he was afterwards allowed to wear a plume. These were made from the hair of a horse's tail, preferably white, which was boiled in water along with a certain root of a plant for many hours causing it to turn a blood red. This horse-hair plume was then fastened to the top of a pointed bamboo hairpin, and as the custom of the Lakher men is to wear their hair in a large overhanging knob at one side of their forehead, this plume when stuck into this knob of hair, falling down the back of the neck, indeed looked formidable, and any one seen wearing this plume, which is called a "*Chhy-thlia,*" was at once looked upon by his fellow-men with dread, knowing that he had been brave enough to capture a head.

The human head, after the "Ia" ceremony, was stuck on to the end of a bamboo some twenty or thirty feet in length, this bamboo being stuck into the ground outside at the entrance to the village and remained there until some storm should dash it to the ground, where it used to remain to be kicked about or trampled upon until at last, broken to pieces, it would ultimately disappear. The Lakhers appear apparently to have never kept the human heads as trophies in their houses as some tribes in other parts of the world are known to do, such as the Dyaks of Borneo.

The Lakhers most emphatically believe in a Human Being being formed of a trinity, that is having a body, a soul and a spirit. The body is believed to die and disappear, while the soul of man can never die, but apparently lives on throughout the ages; but a man who dies a natural death, his body dies and his spirit evidently appears to be captured by the evil spirits, but his soul enters into the "A Thi-pa Khi" and there becomes practically idiotic and enters upon its life there as an infant and gradually grows again to manhood and old age. This naturally brings us to the belief that a man lives more than once upon this earth, for the Lakhers believe that it is probable that human beings have three separate existences on this globe which we call the earth.

A man who dies an unnatural death, having been slain by some wild animal or by a fellow-creature, his spirit and his soul live on in the after-world, his body only dying and decaying, but his soul and spirit enter into the "Saw-Vaw-Khi." His friends who have died a natural death before him and have entered the "A Thi-pa Khi" can by goods, animals, etc., pay to the "Saw-Vaw-Khi" a ransom for his soul, and it will then be allowed to enter the "A Thi-pa Khi" with its friends, but on no account can a living person from this earth redeem the soul of one who dies an unnatural death, but the redemption price must come from the deceased relations of the deceased.

The idea is this. A man who dies a natural death dies of a disease and this disease is believed to come directly from the evil spirits. The special evil spirit for this disease having captured the spirit of the sick man, carries it away far into the jungle and there causes it to undergo hard treatment and hard work, often making it carry exceedingly heavy loads, weighing it down to such an extent that the body which has been left behind suffers extreme exhaustion, the body and the soul only being at that time together.

In order to counteract this treatment of the evil spirits the Lakhers immediately undertake to sacrifice various domestic animals in order to appease the evil spirits. They immediately set to work and place round their huts a little bamboo fence, across which no stranger may step. On the roof of the hut they build a little temple of bamboo sticks, such as a child might build in its play, and at the end of one of these sticks they place a small piece of raw cotton. From this raw cotton they run a thread of cotton right the length of the roof, entering through the side wall and again running down the main post of the building and terminating close beside the dying man. Next the domestic animal is brought. It may be a pig, it may be a gayal, or it may be simply a domestic rooster, according to the special evil spirit to whom the sickness is attributed, and so must the colour be. In the greater majority of cases it would be a pure white bird, spotlessly white and without blemish. The animal is sacrificed generally by the head-man of the house—in any case by one of its members, for the Lakhers own no such things as priests; each man is his own priest and performs all the offices of priesthood himself.

Now an interesting question is this: Why should these wild people sacrifice their domestic animals, which stand for their wealth, to the evil spirits? As I said previously, they firmly believe that an evil spirit has carried away the spirit of the dying man and has inflicted upon it all the trials of a slave, and they believe that by offering this sacrifice this evil spirit will be induced in all probability to let loose the spirit of the dying man.

As soon as the sacrifice is over they take the fruit of the calabash, in the shape of a hollowed out gourd with a hole cut in one end and sometimes in two places, and placing this in their mouth, blowing through it they cause it to make a dull, solemn sound which seems to go through one as a great cry of despair. This is repeated many times during the succeeding twenty-four hours, and the blowing of the gourd is simply to direct the now released spirit of the sick man to his village; but as there is a possibility of the spirit missing the house in which its body lies prostrated, the little bamboo temple with the raw cotton and cotton thread attached is placed on the roof, and this is believed to direct the spirit to its desired haven.

Striking the raw cotton it immediately runs along the cotton thread, following it through the wall, down the main post of the house, and thus once again re-entering the body of the prostrate man, in a very similar way to which we transmit messages one from another by wireless telegraphy. The spirit once more having entered into the prostrate man, he immediately starts to recover, and in a short time is once more restored to health and strength.

It is interesting to note the mode these people have at times of making a promise to evil spirits if they will but answer their requests.

A man or woman lies dying, or at least is seriously ill and unable to move in the dull interior of his hut. The head of the family, which may be either a man or a woman, makes a small string bow and two small arrows feathered with the feathers of a certain coloured domestic fowl, generally white. These weapons are mere toys, very much like one would make for a little child of three or four years old to play with, the bow having power to carry the arrow but a very few yards. Armed with this bow and two arrows, the one allotted will stand just inside the dismal doorway of the hut, glancing suspiciously up and down the little street outside. All at once she will make a sudden rush down the front steps, which are made of a log with nitches cut in it, run out towards the centre of the road and kneeling down will quickly shoot one arrow into the air across the road, which is followed speedily by the second arrow, not a moment having been lost. The instant these two arrows have left the string of the bow she drops her hand on the first two round stones that may be beside her, and jumping quickly up she rushes with all speed into her hut once again. Taking these two stones with her, she places them beside the sick person, saying "These are the two stones that the evil spirit has given me."

This whole ceremony has a very significant meaning, for it is a vow to the evil spirit, and this is the interpretation of it.

The feathers on the arrows were of the same colour and represented the bird to whom they belonged, and in this act of shooting them into the air she has vowed this—*that if the evil spirit will allow the sick person in the hut to get well again she promises most faithfully to give to this evil spirit the life of a domestic fowl, its colour being identical to the colour of the feathers on the arrows.*——

After this little ceremony two or three days elapse, and if the sick person rallies at all and his health commences to return to him the sacrifice will take place as was vowed a day or two previously by the shooting of the arrows.

The relationship of soul and spirit is believed to be so closely allied to one another that in several of the beliefs of the Lakhers in regard to this, their ideas are rather vague, and in some cases it appears that the spirit can die, while in other cases it is believed that at the death of a person his spirit is captured by the evil spirits and needs redemption. This will account for the seeming contradiction in some of the statements in this chapter which are unavoidable.

The re-existence of a soul upon this globe as believed by the Lakhers is interesting, and which I will endeavour to make clear.

A person dies: his spirit is at once captured by the evil spirits and becomes a slave of such until the relations of the deceased who have themselves previously passed in death and have entered the " A Thi-pa Khi " offer certain goods from the abode of the dead to the evil spirits as a redemption for this newly deceased person. When the ransom has been paid the evil spirits are bound to let the spirit of this deceased person go, and he enters into the " A Thi-pa Khi," which is believed to be situated in a far remote corner of the Lakher Country, the road to which leads past a large lake, and many Lakhers (living) declare that as they have passed through a certain portion of that country they have heard the women with their bamboo water-pots and with their axes chopping wood and talking whilst at their work quite distinctly, when no human being has been within many miles of the spot save themselves, and it is believed by them to be the sounds of the working of their relations who have in years past entered into the " A Thi-pa Khi."

The spirit of the deceased having been ransomed by deceased friends of the deceased, enters into the " A Thi-pa Khi " or " Village of the Dead Men," and becomes a child again and grows in the " A Thi-pa Khi " into manhood or womanhood, and thence on to old age once more and at last dies again.

Now when the spirit dies it becomes a cloud, which falls to the earth in the form of an earth-worm (*Cha-ka-ri-pa*). This is the case where the spirits have not been of Royal Blood on our planet. The worm, which is really the spirit from the "A Thi-pa Khi" deceased, lying upon this earth in all probability will be swallowed by a domestic fowl and is digested and passed off in excrement, and in this case the rain falling upon the earth washes it to the river, the river rushes on to the sea, and it is lost for ever. But should a man have killed the fowl and eaten it after it having eaten the worm, or should a man have drunk the water of the river, the spirit is once again reinstated and lives upon this earth in the person of his offspring.

In the case of a deceased spirit having lived previously on this earth with Royal Blood in his veins, the process is a little different. The spirit becoming a cloud it floats through the air until at last it is distilled in rain and dew, which falls upon the various leaves of plants, and if these leaves happen to be eaten by mankind, the spirit once again lives in the form of an offspring. Thus a person who is of Royal Blood upon this earth at the present time, may, on his second existence here, have no Royal Blood in his veins, while on the other hand one of the common people having passed through death may become of Royal Blood if the leaves or the fowl or the water have been demolished by one of the Ruling Clan, and vice versa. Animals having eaten the leaves, the belief is that the only chance of a second existence upon this earth in that case is the drinking of the water by some human being.

The destiny of an infant who dies before it is old enough to know its mother or father is believed to be slightly different: its spirit hovering round near at hand hears, it may be, the rustle of a leaf owing

Lakher village scene. Woman weaving, and trays of rice drying in the sun (*p.* 136).

Lakher children making clay pellets for their bows (*p.* 138).

[To face p. 100.

to the blowing of the wind, and thinking that perhaps it is the voice of its mother or father, cries the cry of a spirit, and God in compassion looks down on it and in some cases carries it away to Heaven, the abode of " Khazopa," and there causes it to become a god to care for the life and preservation of some human being upon the earth, or else it is permitted to have a re-existence upon the earth.

The Lakhers, who are generally termed "Animists," or " Devil Worshippers," should be defined in truer terms as " Devil Appeasers," for they do not in any way worship the evil spirits, but fear them with a great fear, and in order to keep them in a good temper or to appease them from their anger, they sacrifice their various domestic animals to them.

At certain periods, as I mentioned before, they worship God by sacrificing to Him a large pig, the object of which is to call His blessing upon their home that they may have health and strength, for they believe that He wishes them good and is not seeking their hurt as the evil spirits are most emphatically believed to be.

The tiger, too, by certain clans of the Lakhers is much feared as a god, and it is believed by these people that in time gone by their very first parents were changed into tigers. For this reason no Lakher will shoot a tiger without first having offered a very special sacrifice to the evil spirits in order to obtain power over the spirit of this beast which they wish to hunt, and I have seen myself a dead tiger being brought through the village strung on to a pole, and the greater part of the people when they hear of it coming past will not dare look at it, but quickly rush into their hut and shut the door, so that their eyes should not behold the beast.

With these wild hillsmen, every high hill, every large river, every great boulder, every gigantic chasm or large cave, in fact everything that is in any way out of the ordinary, is regarded as the abode of evil spirits. Every valley and a great number of large trees are also supposed to be the abode of evil spirits, while a tree having a hole pierced through its trunk owing to a freak in its formation, or an eyelet-hole in the branch of a tree, or a twisted loop in any vine, on a level with the human eye, that may occur in the jungle, all these are considered to be the abode of evil spirits and are looked on with fear by the Lakhers. Should a man have cut a large cultivation for himself, and towards the end of his work should he discover a tree with one of these holes pierced right through its trunk or branch, he will immediately abandon the whole site and go to some other part of the jungle and start over again, rather than dare cultivate that spot or fell that tree.

Besides the worship of God, the Lakhers at certain times offer worship to the largest mountain within sight of their village, not forgetting to worship any large river, and the Kolodyne river which runs through the country is worshipped by them, and is known to them as the " Beino," which means " Chieftainess." To all these do they offer from time to time the sacrifice of animal and bird life, which in every case belong to the domestic animal family.

When a village is newly built a clear space in the centre of it on flat ground is made and kept for the express purpose of carrying out their religious ceremonies and dances at their huge feasts and sacrificial ceremonials.

The village, however, must be in existence for ten years before a certain species of the Indian fig tree is planted on this clear spot, which is known as the "Tlylia."

On the completion of ten years' residence at this particular site a large feast is called, at which much rice beer is drunk, much dancing takes place, and all the warriors of the tribe, their wives and maidens, are decked up with all the savage tokens and bright head-dresses indicating the valour of their respective owners. A small sapling of a species of Indian fig tree known as the "*Bôchhi*" is procured from the jungle, and with great ceremonial is planted at the further end of the "Tlylia." Three large slabs of stone are then procured from the mountain which it is their habit to worship, and these three stones are arranged at the foot of the newly-planted "Bôchhi," two of them firmly planted as pillars standing upright to a height of about two feet. In front of these two pillars the other slab of stone is placed lying flat with the ground, but buried firmly in it. This slab acts as the altar. After the planting of the "Bôchhi" and the fixing of the sacrificial stones, the sacrifice of some large domestic animal takes place, and the blood and certain portions of it are placed upon this rude altar, whilst the flesh of the animal is eaten of by all those gathered at the feast. These three sacrificial stones are together known as the "Tlylia-lô," and on special occasions, from time to time, sacrifices on this altar will take place to the evil spirit that is believed to preside in the midst of this sacred tree, the "Bôchhi," the tree only being sacred after this ceremony has taken place. Elsewhere the fruit may be picked and eaten and the tree cut about as much as one likes, but when once planted on the "Tlylia" with the sacrificial rites and ceremonies the cutting of the tree in any way is believed to mean death to the perpetrator of the crime or of one of his relatives in his house.

In Sherkor village there is a tree of this description on the "Tlylia" which was a magnificent specimen and had the most luxuriant vegetation, with wide spreading branches covering an exceedingly large area of ground. Every one entering the village could not help but admire the beauty of the tree, but its branches spread over so large an area of space that they became far too weighty for the strength of the trunk and during one of our very severe storms the trunk was snapped near the ground and the tree came crashing down, much to the great terror and consternation of the Lakhers. They were in a terrible plight what to do, believing that it was a sign that some appalling disaster was about to happen to their village.

After a council of war they decided that the only thing they could do was to lop off its branches near the stem and prop it up. This they did, and at a distance of about two feet they erected a strong bamboo fence encircling the trunk filling the receptacle with earth. With the huge branches they had lopped off they made props to form an additional support to the trunk, burying one end in the ground, and every limb of the tree had under it one of these props. The smaller foliage they threw over the precipice close at hand.

I had advised them to throw the whole thing over the precipice, to forsake their heathen custom and to serve and honour the One and Only Living God, "Jehovah." This they were afraid to do, but for some long time they remained in great fear as to the result of this terrible catastrophe as the falling of the "Bôchhi" appeared to them to be, and I used to act rather as a Job's comforter by informing them that God was so very much stronger than the Devil that He had thrown him over and cast him out and wanted to embrace them as His children if they would but turn to Him and cast away their heathen devices.

In course of time the tree started to grow again, and all the branches which had been used as props to support the main trunk also sprouted, with the result that in the place of that once most magnificent and awe-inspiring tree, there stood up a most miserable and dilapidated specimen of a "Bôchhi."

The terrible fear in which these people continually live in regard to evil spirits is appalling. Their whole lives are permeated with the constant thought of avoiding offence towards these much dreaded realities, and in my mind these fears are not without foundation, for the enormous power that evil spirits seem to have over these wild hillsmen is very great, and ofttimes powerfully real.

We who live in a civilized country, and one that has boasted of the name of "Christian" for so many hundred years, cannot in the least degree realize the terrible chains of bondage under which these, our fellow-brethren, are bound, and the longer one lives amongst these most interesting people, the more realistic is the awful power of the Evil One over their lives.

Jesus Christ Himself came to snap every fetter of sin and every fetter wherewith the Evil One has bound His children, and civilization can never snap these chains. There is but one power that is able to cut asunder those links of steel and set the captive free, and that power is the Blood of Jesus Christ, God's Son, Who came into the world to save sinners.

What responsibility rests on each one who bears the Name of Christ, for these wild hillsmen in their jungle homes in the midst of the densest heathen darkness, bound with superstitions and manacles of the Devil's design, are crying for help, for freedom, for liberty, and yet so many of the Children of God are still shutting their ears to the human cry and allowing these multitudes of people to go down into outer darkness without a ray of hope, without the knowledge of the saving power of the Son of God, sparing but the crumbs from their table to feed their dark-skinned brothers with the Unsearchable Riches of Christ, whilst for their own pleasure, for their own glory, for their own gratification, nothing but the very best is sufficient.

To those who have never stood in the midst of heathen darkness, is it nothing that all these countless multitudes of people who are not blessed with the privileges with which we have been blessed, that they should sink into outer darkness, that they should live in the utmost superstition, in the terrible heart-rending fear of evil dignitaries besetting them every day of their lives, is it nothing that they should go down to a heartless grave without a word of comfort at the very mouth of the tomb? And as I have stood many a time by the side of a dying heathen man and asked him what were his hopes, warrior as he had been, animals without number that he had slain and brought low, heads that have fallen under the might of his arm, sacrifices without number that he had made in order to obtain power over these animal and human spirits after death, with all the glory of heathen life, with all the honours of the Lakher plume, after all the ceremonies and sacrifices that have prompted his life, with his vows and the fulfilment of those vows to the evil spirits ;—I say when I have stood beside his miserable couch, filthy in most cases to the extreme, with the air thick with the smoke from an open grate and a wood fire flickering in the hearth throwing weird shadows o'er the dying man and those dark-skinned friends of his sitting by drinking at the beer pot and talking at the top of their voices discussing what they will do with him as soon as he is dead, how much beer there shall be to drink and where his grave should be dug, and what animal shall be sacrificed that its spirit may accompany his spirit to the great beyond ;—when I have stood by a bed of that sort I have looked the man full in the face and I have asked him, "What is your hope ?"—"What are your prospects ?"—"What is coming ?"—"Have you any joy looming on the other side of death's river for you ?" and in every instance I have been met with the same answer, "NONE,"—"Everything before me is blank,—Terrible darkness,—There is no light,—I see nothing before me but a blank, black darkness."

And then I have spoken to him of the Love of Jesus Christ, of His dying on Calvary that he might live, and pointed him to the Son of God upon the Cross that shed His blood for the ransom of his sin, and pleaded with him to look and live. I have told him of Jesus Christ, the resurrected, Who is soon, so soon, coming again to receive all that love Him to Himself. I have bid him in simple faith accept Jesus Christ as the Son of God, the Saviour, to repent of his sins and ask forgiveness, and ask that he might see Life; and then falling down on my knees before the dying man, have offered up a prayer for him, whilst those that sat around at the beer pot and encircling the fire would stop their talking and listen for a few minutes, for they can never understand how a man can comfort and care much for the dying, then I have had to leave him and go my way, while he has passed beyond recall and gone to his reward.

We are not told in the Holy Scriptures what is the ultimate end of the heathen, but we know that God is just and those that should be beaten with few stripes shall receive few, and those that shall be beaten with many stripes shall receive many. And here we leave him, but he is not an isolated case. Thousands are passing away daily with the same terrible darkness before their eyes. Cannot you, my reader, consecrate your money, your time and your talents, your all, that one stream of light may pierce that terrible darkness, the true light of the Son of God?

Dying, yes, dying in thousands, a heedless, despairing death;
Can we not hear them crying, pleading with bated breath?
"Will no one come over and give us the light;
Must we perish in darkness, darker than night?"

Dying in cruel bondage, with none to set them free,
Though the chains of ignorance and sin are galling so bitterly.
The Saviour has freed us all we know,
Yet no man careth to tell them so.

Dying! Ah! it is easy, unheeding the Master's call,
To sit with folded arms and sing, "Oh! Crown Him Lord of all";
But where are the gems to lay at His feet,
That shall sparkle some day in His Crown complete?

"All power is given unto Me. Go thou into all the world and preach the Gospel," thus saith the Lord. Will you send that ray of light? Will you help to pierce that terrible darkness? You have said you are crucified with Christ. Are you paying the price of that crucifixion, or have you neglected to sanctify your wealth, your all, to the One Who did not neglect to purchase your salvation even at the enormous cost of His Precious Life?

The darkness on the deathbed of a heathen man is terrible, and beyond all imagination. There is but One who can pierce that darkness, break its power, shine through it and save, and He calls you to occupy until He come, to send His Light to the uttermost parts of the world, to send one beam of light at least to some lost soul.

The world is dark, but you are called to brighten
Some little corner, some secluded glen.
Somewhere a burden rests that you may lighten,
And thus reflect the Master's Love for men.

CHAPTER IX

FOOD AND THE DEVIL

IN a former chapter was mentioned about the great similitude in the characteristics of the dress of the men and the women of the Lushai tribes to such an extent that to a newcomer it was practically impossible for them to distinguish between a man and a woman.

This, however, is not the case with the Lakhers, although a photograph of a Lakher man I find from experience gives the idea to the Westerner that he is a woman, yet were one to travel in the country no such error would be made, for the Lakher men and the Lakher women dress with entire distinction from one another.

Both have long, jet-black hair, which when combed out hangs far below the waist, and is almost daily greased with pig's fat, giving it a glossy, oily appearance. In the case of the man this long hair is twisted into a large knob in the front of the head overhanging the forehead, slightly to one side, and is decorated with various hair-pins of brass and of bamboo, the latter very cleverly japanned and decorated. The hair of the man is tidy to the extreme, and gives to him a superior appearance. The hair of the woman is by no means so often greased with pig's fat, and is tied in a loose knot at the nape of the neck, leaving the ends hanging down the back in a very slovenly, unkempt condition, while a huge brass hair-pin, as a rule, keeps the knot in position.

The men wear a small loin cloth, and this, with a string of beads, during the hot weather, comprises their whole attire, whilst during the cold season they wear a large sheet of their own manufacture, having two black stripes running through it, passing under one arm and thrown over the other shoulder, hanging down loosely to their feet.

The young unmarried women wear a petticoat reaching from their waist down to their ankles, which is formed of one length of cloth about six feet in length wound tightly round them, looking uncommonly like a hobble skirt, and is kept in position by an ornamented belt of various patterns; while where a person is too poor to afford a metal belt they wear a belt made of grass, very cleverly plaited and of artistic design. Besides this they wear a short breast-jacket with a sailor collar opening in the front, no sleeves, and reaching just low enough to cover the breasts, whilst the jacket at the back is open, only being kept in place by two pieces of twine tied into a knot at the back, for a Lakher cannot tie a bow.

Both the petticoat and the breast-jacket are of exceedingly pretty designs, most cleverly woven with their primitive weaving looms. The married women, after their first child, as a rule, cast off the breast-jacket, and either go with the body above the waist in a nude condition around the village, or else when they go into the jungle to fetch their wood or their water, wear a white cloth coat with sleeves, covering the whole of the bare part of the body. The white jacket is worn for the greater part as a protection against the evil spirits, fearing that should the evil spirits perceive that they have given birth to an offspring, they may sweep down upon the little one at home, cause it to sicken and die. The same custom is followed by a woman who expects soon to become a mother, with the same idea. It is therefore, as a rule, safe to assume that where a female is not wearing the small breast-jacket she is a married woman, and that where the small breast-jacket is worn she is not married.

The colour of the skin of the Lakhers is a dark chocolate-brown. They have rather high cheek bones and brown eyes which are slightly almond-shaped. They live entirely by their agriculture and by hunting, and in years gone by have been great and skilful hunters and warriors, and were one to pass through their village to-day they would find on the verandah wall of every hut dozens of skulls representing almost every wild animal known in the country, from the elephant down to the monkey; but strange to say nowhere will you find the skull of a tiger decorating their houses, whilst the bear and the alligator are often met with. The elephant's skull, however, being of such an enormous size that it did not allow of being carried home, the bone into which the tusks are embedded alone is kept, and these one will find tied up on the front wall of the owners' hut at the back of the verandah.

"Thylai," the Chief of Sherkor, for instance, can boast of having shot no less than ten full-grown elephants, and these huge bones take up a large space of the wall of the verandah, whilst above them and at their side range skulls of wild gayal, Samber deer, bears, and the alligator. All these animals have been killed by means of the flint-lock gun, which requires no little pluck in firing, as they have to be very heavily charged with gunpowder in order to kill these large animals, and ofttimes the barrel explodes when in use, wounding severely and sometimes causing the death of the owner.

The weapons in the possession of the Lakhers, besides the flint-lock gun, are not very numerous, and probably the spear, the bow and pellet, the "Takô" (a kind of large chopper), with a short cutlass very much after the style of the Burmese, will constitute the list.

These people are very ingenious, and although blacksmiths are very rare throughout the country, yet in a village here and there you will find a man skilled in this most useful art. They can make every part of a gun with the exception of the barrel: these alone have they had to secure through barter with native traders to the South, while the hammer, springs and all the mechanism which the gun contains has been carefully forged by themselves from old pieces of scrap iron which they have in one way or another obtained, probably in the form of cooking utensils and knives from these native traders. The butt of the gun is carved out of a solid piece of hard wood, exceedingly artistically decorated, japanned with black and red japan obtained from the juice of trees in the country, and the whole article when completed forms a weapon worthy of the owner. Iron and steel seem to be the only articles for which they are dependent upon the outside world. Practically all the other necessities of life are obtained by their own ingenuity from the products of their own country. They make their own gunpowder, the only part of which they cannot obtain in their own land being the sulphur, and the saltpetre they obtain through a very clever method from the earth underneath their houses.

Their farming implements are exceedingly primitive, the "Takô" being a weapon of defence as well as their implement for building their houses and their plough. Besides this instrument they have a little hoe, and these two articles, with a few bamboo baskets, form all that is necessary for cultivating the ground.

They have a most primitive way also of cultivation. Going out into the jungle a tract of land covered with bamboo is selected where the soil is suitable, and setting to work they cut every bamboo at about two feet from the ground; at each sweep of the Takô a bamboo falls. These bamboos are felled in order, so that one falls upon another in the same position, and a man will continue from sunrise to sunset to steadily cut these hundreds and thousands of bamboos down, each one falling upon its neighbour. Thus he will continue for ten days. At the end of ten days' work a sufficient amount of land is cleared to support one family when cultivated. The bamboos by this time are probably lying on the land six or eight feet deep and these are left in this condition for a month or six weeks under the tropical sun during the dry season. When they become thoroughly dry, which is towards the end of March, he takes a torch, and going down to the valley—for all these cultivations are cut on the steep hill-sides—he sets alight these dried bamboos in several places, after which he rushes away with all speed from the spot. The bamboos being so exceedingly dry, aided by the great heat of the tropical sun, the flames soon spread, and licking up the dried bamboos, the whole hillside is in a very few minutes one mass of huge flames, burning everything before it, leaving the whole mass of débris reduced to ashes.

As soon as it is possible to stand on these ashes without burning the feet, planting begins, and the man in a squatting position, by means of his Takô, scratches a little hole in the ashes and earth, dropping in a few grains of rice and Indian corn, and also various other seeds, which have to form the mainstay of his family during the coming twelvemonth.

It being too much trouble for them to cover these seeds over with earth after they are dropped into these little holes, they leave this process to the most obliging rain which they know will speedily follow at this time of the year, for the cultivation is never set alight until they see the gathering clouds of a storm in the sky. The rain pours down, washes the ashes and the mould over the seeds, and the setting of their cultivation is complete. In due course these seeds germinate to life and the whole hillside is one mass of green, which grows very rapidly under the heavy rains that fall during the rainy season.

There is very little order to these cultivations. Indian corn, rice, Job's tears, millet, cucumbers, melons, pumpkins and the calabash are all mixed up together and grow as they will, but along with these spring up the weeds very speedily, far quicker indeed than the true grain, and the process of weeding their cultivations soon commences.

Twice during the rainy season are they obliged to weed the whole of their cultivations ere the crop is ripe and ready to harvest. This weeding is a tedious undertaking, and is done by means of the Takô and the small hoe to which reference has been made, the whole family, both male aud female, helping in the work, but the women do not have to do more of this weeding work than is absolutely necessary to keep under the weeds and undergrowth.

At the end of July the maize crop is ready to harvest, and it is to this crop that the Lakhers look for help to enable them to get through the year without starvation. Their land not being very fertile, they are unable to grow sufficient rice to last them the whole of the twelve months. Towards the end of October the firstfruits of the rice harvest is picked, and during the end of November and beginning of December as a rule the whole of the rice crop is harvested while for several months past they have been eating the fruit of the cucumber, the pumpkin and various other vegetables, including the cultivated yam and the "Bia," a species of arum lily bulb which practically takes the place of the potato in the country and is excellent eating, although if too much of it is indulged in one is liable to suffer from violent pains in the abdomen.

In the centre of each cultivation is erected a little farmhouse which is made of bamboo and is really a small hut built on piles. In this house the people often spend the best part of the rainy season, during which time they are very busy on their cultivations, the whole family leaving the village and going out to this little farmhouse for several months at a stretch and not returning to the village again until the whole of the crops are harvested. Another little hut is also built which is comprised of a floor with a roof over it, built on piles, and no walls, but on this floor are erected large bins, the sides of which are made of split bamboos and lined with leaves, and in these bins the gathered grain is placed. The

Lakher farm and farm-house with family (p. 116).

The aged wife of a Lakher Chief making clay pots (p. 142).

[*To face p.* 116.

maize crop, however, is gathered in cob, and the cobs are tied together and suspended on bamboos under the roof of the hut in which they live, the smoke of the fire helping to dry and preserve them from the numerous insects who love to feast on them.

The mode of harvesting with the Lakhers is of great interest. When the rice is ready to be gathered in, they pull the whole plant up by the roots, place a great number of them together and bind them into a sheaf, placing the sheaf against some charred stump of a bamboo which they have left sticking out all over the cultivation at the time of their cutting it, and which has not been entirely burnt down to the ground. In this manner they remain for a week or ten days in order that they may get thoroughly ripened by the tropical sun. After this the men and women with baskets on their backs go round to each sheaf and cut off the heads of the grain, throwing the precious grain into the basket and leaving the straw behind to rot. When this is all gathered in they place it in large piles upon the floor on a very finely-woven bamboo mat, or, weather permitting, a part of the ground is cleared outside the huts and used as the threshing-floor. Then, standing upon these large piles of grain with their naked feet, continually moving from morning till night they tread out the grain until at last the outside husks and stems are separated from the real grain in husk. The true grain is then placed on large bamboo-matted trays and the women are very skilful in tossing these trays with a certain motion to clear away any husks or small stems that may be left, after which the tray full of true grain is placed in the large bins which are in the hut close at hand. When the whole of the harvest is completed, walls are built round the granary and the door is securely fastened, so that any attempt by an outsider to rob another of his grain will speedily be detected and the offender caught.

After this is all completed the family once more return to their village to take up their abode for the dry season, and many feasts and ceremonies are gone through in thanks for the harvest which they have reaped, large beer drinks being organized and much of the new rice being used in the brewing of this rice beer, with the result that for several weeks to come nothing but the sounds of beer drinks and the sight of men enlivened by the power of the drink, with many a savage fight and many an unpleasant sound, continue day and night for many days in succession.

The Lakhers have a very interesting custom which goes by the name of "Ria-lô-chhi," which is a ceremony for dedicating their implements to their farm use. First of all the fruit of the hog-plum ("Dokao") is gathered, and these are carefully brought home and eaten, while the stones inside of them are carefully preserved. They next take a bow and an arrow, piercing the stone of the hog-plum with the point of the arrow so that it is firmly fixed on the arrow head. They next place this stone in the fire, and very soon it is all alight, and while it is in this burning condition they carry it into the open in the front of their huts, and placing the arrow into the string of the bow they fire it into the air and the flame from the hog-plum stone goes whizzing into space like fireworks. As each arrow is fired and each streak of light illuminates the air, those joining in the ceremony cheer, and this is supposed to cause the Takô and their little hoe to be of more service and better equipped for the work of farming during the season. This ceremony generally takes place immediately after the cultivations have been cut and before the seeding of the grain commences.

Another very interesting custom is that which goes by the name of "Chaka-lai," and which is a ceremony to drive out famine from the household. When this ceremony is to be carried out the head of the household takes a large flaming firebrand out of the fire inside his hut, rushes to the door and slides it swiftly back, and then singing out these words :—

Chaka si la,
Cha phao si la,
Hia kha tlô la,
Thla-tla tlô la,—

he throws the flaming firebrand into the air in front of the hut, and the ceremony is completed.

This is supposed to drive out famine from the household. He has previously borrowed much rice and other produce from his neighbours in order to enable him to live owing to some unfortunate circumstance that may have arisen in regard to his farming, and according to Lakher custom this borrowed produce must be paid back in double the quantity to that which has been borrowed. After this ceremony has been gone through, however, the borrower is only bound to pay back the same quantity of grain and produce that he previously borrowed, instead of double the amount. A man, however, cannot simply perform this ceremony in order to escape his liabilities of paying double the amount he has borrowed, but there are certain and very rigid conditions laid down between themselves, and only under very special circumstances and by the consent of those concerned, and with that of their Chief, can this ceremony of the "Chaka-lai" be performed.

As soon as the Lakher has built his farmhouse in the midst of his cultivation, and the crops start to appear above the ground, in little patches among the grain, and especially around his farmhouse close at hand he plants a little seed which soon springs up and which flowers during the time that the grain commences to ripen. Its flower is of bright red, is extremely beautiful to behold, and falls as if it were a fountain of blood issuing from the common stem of the plant. This flower has a particular virtue according to their ideas, for they claim that were it not for this flower being planted on their cultivations the evil spirits would be able to see them at their work and would do them great harm, if not actually kill them; but this red flower, growing as it does here and there all over the cultivation, comes between them and the evil spirits and protects them.

Surely here we have a wonderful suggestion of the Precious Blood of Jesus Christ which comes between the sinner and his sin, which frees him, protects him, keeps him, so that all those who have accepted the Blood of Jesus Christ as a redemption for their sin are no more under the power of the Evil One; and we trust, and pray, and work, that the day may come when these wild Lakher hillsmen may realize that they not only have the blood-red flower of this beautiful plant between them and the Evil One, but that the True and Precious Blood of Jesus Christ is keeping and supporting them from all the powers of the Devil, not only on their farms but when they travel from village to village, when far away from home, or at home, with no visible sign, but a power through Faith to see that Wonderful Crimson Fountain that flowed for them from Calvary.

The Lakher language is a strange tongue, but stranger still perhaps is the knowledge that the people when passing through the jungle and talking to one another about their various domestic animals, their increase, or their decrease may be, which really amounts to talking about their wealth or poverty, they never use the ordinary Lakher equivalents for their domestic animals. The gayal, the pig, the goat, the fowls, would not be called by their proper names for fear that the evil spirits would hear and understand what they were talking about, and would immediately set their hatred upon them and revenge themselves by causing their domestic animals to speedily die.

For instance, instead of calling a *gayal* a "Sei" they would use the word "Rabapa" (jungle eater), and instead of calling a *pig* a "Vao" they use the word "Sah-hro" (live animal), and instead of calling a *goat* a "Mi" they will call it "Tho-hna-pa" (medicine), and instead of calling a domestic *fowl* an "Aw" they use the word "Pavaw" (bird). This is done entirely with the idea of misleading the evil spirits, and if you should be going through the jungle with a number of these people and should happen to use the proper words for these domestic animals, they will immediately hush your speech with a "Sh—sh—!" and their minds will become full of agitation unless you speedily correct yourself.

It is surprising to find how exceedingly foolish the Lakhers consider the evil spirits to be as shown by many of their customs, for ofttimes when sickness is rampant in a Lakher village, as you walk round you will see suspended from the roof of the hut in front of the verandah a single large leaf of a particular plant hanging by a fine piece of cane tied to the stalk of this leaf, which has previously been pierced with a great number of holes. The wind as it blows causes the leaf to spin round, and the holes in the leaf look uncommonly like many eyes. This is supposed to frighten the evil spirits, which are believed to cause the sickness in the village, from climbing up their front log stairway and entering into their hut and smiting some one or other with the dread disease.

Another devil frightener which is often resorted to, suspended in the same manner from the same position, is the effigy of a Lakher man made from the shavings of the bamboo, which is very carefully tied and twisted and makes a most curious-looking being. In his hand is a bow to which an arrow is fixed, and he is in the attitude of letting it fly from his bow string. This also is believed to make the evil spirits afraid to enter.

When a village is attacked by some epidemic an archway of bamboo is built at the entrance to the village, and hundreds upon hundreds of short, pointed bamboos are placed up the sides and over the top and all along the fence at the side of this archway with their sharp points sticking out towards the jungle, looking exceedingly formidable, and the entrance being very narrow, one has to take great care when on pony back not to run into them, as they would inflict a very severe wound.

Ofttimes over this doorway and at the sides many of these curious images made of bamboo shavings may be seen in all manner of attitudes, and some of them exceedingly hideous to look upon.

When this is completed the village calls upon a three days' separation, and a bamboo doorway, also containing a great number of sharpened bamboo spikes, closes up the roadway, and no stranger is allowed to enter the village during these three days, and no person in the village is allowed to go out during the same period, whilst in the village itself many houses will undertake to offer special sacrifices; and the sacrifice of a domestic fowl also is offered and hung up on a stick just outside this gateway at the close of the three days. This is an offering to the evil spirits which are believed to be round the precincts of the village at this time. The gate is then taken down and thrown away, but the archway remains until at last it decays and rots away and falls down of itself; it is never pulled down by human hands, and this special ceremony of separation is believed to cause the epidemic to leave their village for good.

During our sojourn in Sherkor such an epidemic broke out and great numbers of the people died. We were, however, enabled to save a large number of lives we believe, not alone through our medical treatment but through the blessing which God gave us in the use of medicine. For a long time one heard nothing but the doleful boom of their huge gongs, the noise of heavy beer-drinking bouts, the sound of their long, solemn and heart-rending chants, day in and day out, throughout the day and throughout the night, until it was indeed a most heart-rending time.

A man would die and he would be kept in his hut, decorated according to their custom, for a period as long as five days, whilst on the verandah outside the hut and also on the inside of the hut large numbers of the relatives and friends would be gathered drinking beer, chanting their chants and talking one against the other at the top of their voices, the greater part of them being in a state of savage drunkenness.

In a country as hot as Lakherland, the bodies of the dead cannot be kept longer at the most than about thirty-six hours, and even then the body has started to give off offensive odours, but at the end of the five days the stench is almost unbearable. The consequence was that those who attended these "wakes" were soon stricken down themselves and great numbers of them died, the same thing happening over and over again, over the various bodies, and the epidemic seemed to take a great hold on the people; but it was a marvellous thing to find that every case of sickness which cared to take the medicines which we offered instead of sacrificing to the evil spirits, recovered, and during that most solemn time it was our privilege not to lose one patient whom we had the opportunity of treating, while many of those who refused our treatment, preferring to resort to their sacrifices to appease the evil spirits, passed away.

The ceremony which I spoke of above was then called for and was duly performed, and strange to say that after the ceremony was over and the gate had been taken and thrown away, the archway and fence still remaining for a great number of months, the epidemic decreased and very shortly after vanished altogether, and Sherkor was once more restored to health.

In numerous cases where the evil spirits have been appeased by these people and special sacrifices have been offered to appease them, I have noticed that it has been very effective, and it appears to me that all these strange customs in regard to devil-appeasing worship are not to be pooh-poohed. A great deal is very absurd and mere child's play, but there is a part of it which from experience makes me feel that there is a great reality, to some extent at any rate, and when we think of all these people bound in the chains of the Evil One, slaves to the Devil who has such an enormous power over them, surely it is feasible to believe that the Devil, whose servants they are, will hearken to their cry and relieve them from the terrible obligations that are often placed upon them. But although they may be saved from these physical difficulties for the time being through the offering of sacrifices of animals and birds, the Evil One receiving the life of the animal or bird as the case may be, and yet still holding the power over the human spirit, only saves them for a time and not for eternity, and who realizes better than the Evil One himself that at the death of his servants he shall claim their souls for eternal ruin.

But the power of the Gospel of Jesus Christ not only snaps every fetter which the Evil One has placed round these dark-skinned brothers of ours, but it saves them from his power and his might; and what is more it saves their souls throughout all eternity, and gives them the hope, the blessed hope, of a life hereafter in the presence of their God.

No sooner than these Lakhers give their hearts to Jesus Christ, throw up their sacrifices to the evil spirits and follow Him alone, stepping out upon His promise, believing that He has paid the penalty of sin through the sacrifice of Himself on Calvary's tree, and that His blood has saved and does save, as soon as they realize that, and step out upon His promise, the whole power of the Evil One appears to be cut asunder; whilst their fellow men are under the bondage of the evil spirits, they stand as it were as an island stands, in the midst of the sea, surrounded by the mighty ocean of power which cannot be crossed by legions of evil spirits and their Prince.

Another circumstance stands out most clearly before our eyes. Lakher tribesmen will come to our Mission School. They have been appeasing the evil spirits all their lives, but they come to school to learn to read and write, but deeper down than that they come with the curiosity of learning what God says. They enter our school for twelve months' study, and during that time they live within the boundary of our compound. No one is allowed to offer a sacrifice to an evil spirit whilst under our supervision, and in every way possible their connection with heathendom is practically cut off. What is the result? Up to the present time we have never had any sickness amongst our scholars. They have become greatly improved in health and each one of them realizes in their mind that whilst under our Christian influence they are protected from the power of the evil spirits, and I believe that this is purely through the power of God Who has surrounded, does surround, and will surround His work and His workers with a wall which the Devil and his angels may never pass over without His permission, as was the case with the life of Job, for there we are distinctly taught that the Evil One himself can only touch the Children of God after having obtained permission of the Father, and can never overstep the limitations which the Father Himself lays down.

Where, however, there is no knowledge of the Saving Power of Jesus Christ it is an entirely different thing, none to protect, no wall of separation around, no limitations laid down, but absolutely under the power and control, under the supervision and command of the hard task master and his embassy.

Once take the knowledge of this great wall, the fortification of the soul, Jesus Christ, to these people, make them realize the power thereof, work with that end in view, sacrifice one's self in order that they may realize the truth of such salvation, and allow the Holy Spirit to teach, to lead gently but surely, little by little, day by day, and the power of the Devil and his legions must dwindle away. These great fortresses of darkness in Lakherland must fall. These mighty forts of the Evil One must crumble to dust. This large tract of country containing range upon range of hills, stretching from North to South, dotted here and there with the villages of this raw heathen tribe, from whose summits and valleys nothing but the heathen chants had ever swelled, must and shall burst forth into praises to Jehovah, the Devil and his legions put to flight, and temples of the rarest beauty reared in the hearts of these simple people who have for so many centuries been bound with the chains of ignorance and sin, and all, not through human power, but by the Almighty Power of God through His Son Jesus Christ, working through those who have been adopted into the family of the living God.

Consecrated lives, consecrated intellect, consecrated wealth are the instruments through which the Lord doth work, not through the gift of those who have never missed what they have given, but through a life so consecrated that all that they have is realized to belong to Him Who gave it and Whose stewards they are, and who give towards the Cause of God to the extent of feeling the amount of the gift, for God looks not upon the amount of the gift so much as He looks upon the amount which has been kept back.

If Christian men and Christian women were but to realize this more fully there would not be a nation or tribe upon the face of this earth who would not have heard of the name and the power to save of Jesus Christ, and thus the Second Appearing of our Lord and Master would be hastened and the joy and expectation of the Church realized.

> Were all the realms of nature mine
> That were an offering far too small,
> Love so amazing, so divine
> Demands my life, my soul, my all.

CHAPTER X

HOME AND HEARTH

THE villages in the Lakher country are always built on the mountain peaks, and the road lying between each village varies from ten to twenty miles in distance, and is as much as one can accomplish in a day's march; pony, rider and carriers all being much fatigued on arrival.

Arriving at a Lakher village, what are the general everyday day scenes which surround one, how do the people live, and what occupies their time from morning till night? is what one would naturally wish to know. I have spoken of the labour entailed in cultivating the land, such land being situated at a distance from the village, but passing that aside let us see what their village life is like.

Women and men have their own distinct work, and both classes are brought up from early childhood to endure the burden of heavy loads supported on their foreheads by the proverbial cane-strap and cord with the load resting on the back.

Having arrived at the Lakher village, our only abode is the humble hut of the villager, and the people are extremely kind in this particular. A family in the best and cleanest hut in the village will willingly turn out for the night in order that the "Mongyupa" (white man) may have a night's shelter. In front of the hut is a large verandah, upon which we shall find a pile of split wood for the fire; a number of baskets ranged round the walls where the domestic fowls lay their eggs; and at the side of the house under the eaves of the roof a large bamboo basket of cigar-shape is fixed where the domestic fowls every evening enter and roost together, Lakher fowls never perching on perches but standing on the bamboo matting of a basket, and when night comes the mistress of the house carefully closes the door of this fowl house to protect it from the numerous wild jungle and civet cats that are prowling around in great numbers.

The door of the hut is at the further end of the verandah, and ere we enter we find that the front wall is practically covered with the skulls of numerous animals that have been captured or shot in the chase by the occupant. These are very firmly tied with cane ties to the wall, and indicate to each visitor the prowess of the owner. Sliding back the bamboo door we have to step over a threshold about a foot and a half in height, at the same time ducking our head to save ourselves getting a blow on the forehead from the top of the door, which is very small.

On entering the hut we find there are no windows, and the only light that is to be obtained within has to come through the walls themselves where the bamboo matting has not been firmly knocked together, and naturally inside such a place as this everything seems very dark, until after a few minutes in the interior, when one is able to discern the various articles of furniture, which is very scanty.

We find close beside us towards the centre of the hut a fireplace formed of clay about six inches in depth and surrounded with split logs to prevent this clay from getting chipped and broken up. In the centre of this fireplace are three stones fitted so that a pot may rest upon them, and between these three stones the sticks are laid and the fire lit. At each corner of this primitive fireplace is a pole reaching up to the roof, and about five feet above the fire is a mantelpiece formed of matted bamboo, under which skewers of meat are seen to be drying in the smoke, and it may be a number of fish also are placed there to dry. On the top of this mantelpiece is a large tray containing unhusked rice, which is also placed there in order that the husk may get separated from the grain and be easier for pounding and cleansing when needed. The fire sends a weird glimmer round the hut, the smoke curls up to the mantelpiece, causing the bamboo matting to become an ebony black with a highly polished surface, but everything is covered with soot. The whole of the roof of the hut, which is formed of leaves, is hanging with soot several inches in length. The meat and fish which are smoking in the smoke of this fire are also covered with soot, and the whole atmosphere of the hut is one mass of smoke, causing the eyes very quickly to smart to those who have not yet become used to it.

Along the side of the hut, which is a roomy one, are several bamboo shelves upon which clay pots of various sizes, little bamboo baskets and various other little articles for household use are arranged, while in one corner you will find a large bamboo bin in which the rice in husk is kept for immediate use.

During the time of the Indian corn crop the whole of the roof of the hut is often decorated with the Indian corn cobs, keeping exceedingly well for a number of months whilst remaining in the smoke of the fire which kills the numerous insects that love to attack it, but needless to say the rats accumulate and eat a great amount of this corn, and they also make an exceedingly great noise of a night, scampering as they do over these cobs of grain, making it almost impossible for a stranger to get a wink of sleep.

In another corner of the hut a large basket may be seen in which the cotton thread, both white and black, is kept, and on the wall close by we shall find a weaving loom made very primitively from a few sticks of bamboo. A few weapons also may be found sticking in the wall, a spear, a *takô* or small chopper, an axe, several bows and a bag of pellets for use with the same.

By the side of the fireplace we may find a bed of bamboo raised above the floor at a height of only about three inches, but in many of the huts this bed is absolutely dispensed with and the occupants sleep on the floor itself, which is raised from the ground, every hut being built on piles, the door sometimes being level with the ground in front or only slightly raised, but at the back of the hut there will be a ten to twenty feet drop, as these houses are all built on the hillsides.

At the back of the hut we find a partition running nearly the whole way across. Passing through to the other side we find a little door which opens out at the back of the hut and looks out into space. Occasionally a platform will be found outside at this end, but in the majority of cases the door simply looks out into space without a platform outside. Behind this little partition is á latrine, and this is a custom which is followed only by the Lakhers and is not practised by any of the neighbouring tribes.

In this primitive abode we take up our residence

for the night, and there being no tables or chairs the little camp table and camp chairs have to be brought out, whilst a camp cot forms our bed, being covered up with a mosquito net more for the purpose of keeping the dust and rats off of one than for keeping mosquitos away, as the smoke from the fire in our dingy quarters does not allow these tiresome pests to enter the building.

Underneath the hut the domestic animals live: gayal, pigs, goats and cows, and maybe the missionaries' own ponies are also picketed underneath, and at an exceedingly early hour, long before the day has started to break, the grunts of the pigs, the crowing of the cockerels and the cackling of the hens, the baying of the gayal, will rob one of all sleep, the only remedy being to bestir one's self as quickly as possible; and it is an exceedingly common thing for the hut to receive many violent shakes during the night from the huge gayal which ofttimes scratch their backs against the piles, giving one the idea that they are experiencing a terrible earthquake.

Before the dawn of day has set in a heavy thud! thud! thud! will be heard issuing from every hut throughout the village, and on going outside to see what is happening we find that two women from each of the families are already busy pounding their rice in their primitive pestle and mortar.

The pestle is formed by a long piece of hard wood about six feet in length, while the mortar is the trunk of a tree hollowed out at one end to receive the grain. The women standing on either side of this mortar, each with a pestle in hand, strike the unhusked grain in rotation, and as the grain spins to one side of the mortar she very cleverly throws it back with her toe as the pestle from her companion comes down with great force within a hair's breadth of smashing it. So proficient are they at this work that during our long sojourn amongst these people I have only known of one woman having received a blow on her toe from the pestle.

After the pounding has proceeded for the space of about twenty minutes, the grain is taken out, thrown on to a bamboo tray and in a very cunning manner is winnowed, the chaff being separated from the true grain and being cast off into a basket, while the true grain is placed into another basket, afterwards to be placed into a clay pot with water and cooked on the primitive fireplace for the morning meal of the family, while the husks are cooked for the pigs. Winnowing is a very clever art of the women, and the male portion of the people are unable to perform it.

As soon as the pot is boiling on the fire the women take their basket, place it on their backs, and going to the corner of the hut pick out all their bamboo water-pots that may be empty, and placing them in their baskets they make their way to the spring in the valley, taking in their hands at the same time their cotton thread and spindles which are to occupy their time along the road, a custom which women in Lakherland are prone to follow, thus occupying their time even while travelling from one place to another.

The water fetched, which is a heavy load, probably consisting of ten or twelve bamboo water-pots, weighing perhaps when full of water sixty pounds or more, and the morning meal being cooked, it is turned out on to a large wooden plate and the whole household squat round on their haunches in a circle, each helping themselves from a common dish with their hands, thrusting the morsels into their mouth with a peculiar side jerk which is very cleverly performed, with very few particles falling to the ground and without the hands becoming very sticky with the food.

At times various leaves boiled in the form of a vegetable will be eaten with their rice, and the Lakhers are always happy with these two articles of food if there is plenty of salt to go with it—an article which they much appreciate and which is very beneficial to their health. A piece of smoked pig's flesh, however, is greatly appreciated and will cause them to have a greater appetite for their frugal meal, but ofttimes flesh is not available, and the people as a rule live wholly upon rice or Indian corn, varying it from time to time with various vegetables such as edible leaves, pumpkins, the yam, or sweet potato when procurable, and with the fruit of the plantain.

As soon as the morning meal is over during the busy season, the male portion of the family wend their way to their various labours, which may be on the farm, or it may be that they are going to occupy their time in hunting or in some improvement of their dwelling.

The women, taking their axes and baskets, march away in companies in Indian file into the jungle to gather wood for the daily fire, for the fire in a Lakher hut is not allowed to go out from one year's end to another. Towards noon the women return with their heavy loads of wood, which they throw down outside their huts, then with their axe very cleverly split the large pieces up into convenient sizes, and this is soon stacked away on their verandahs and the noonday meal is cooked and eaten. The weaving loom is then brought out, and with cotton grown and manufactured by themselves they make some very pretty cloths, decorating them very artistically with various beautiful designs, some of their cloths taking them many months to complete, sometimes a year or more. Red, black, yellow and gold are the general colours employed in the making of this cloth, but the gold is always silk, procured from a silk moth not by the Lakhers themselves but by the hillsmen over the Burmese frontier, who once a year pass through the country in order to barter away the silk which they have obtained.

Weaving is a very tedious occupation, and the women show great skill and patience in their undertakings, the threads of the cloth being very carefully arranged. They obtain their black dye from the indigo plant which they cultivate, while their red and yellow cotton is obtained by boiling the white cotton with various roots dug in the jungle.

The cotton plant is grown upon their cultivations, and they make out of wood an instrument similar to a mangle for seeding the same, the raw cotton passing through the rollers and the cotton seeds in this way being pushed out. After the cotton has been seeded they flick it out with a bow made of bamboo and a taut string, which they keep on flicking against the cotton, causing it to become like down. This down-like cotton is then carded, that is rolled out with the hands into pencil-shaped rolls of about six to nine inches long.

After this another instrument is then brought into use, a wheel made of wood around which

An old Lakher woman winding her cotton thread into balls (*p.* 137).

Lakher maiden seeding her cotton (*p.* 138).

[*To face p.* 136.

a string acting as a band is placed, the other end of it encircling a rounded piece of wood on the end of a steel pin. As the handle of the wheel is turned so the steel pin revolves at a great rate, and in a very clever manner the carded cotton is touched against this steel spindle and is drawn out into thread. This thread, however, is not of sufficient strength to be of any use. It is therefore tied on to the end of a bamboo, which is weighted at one end by a disc of bone from the foot of the elephant, and this is the article with which one will see a woman when on her way to the jungle to fetch wood or water, carrying in her hand and spinning the weighted bamboo round, at the same time running her fingers nimbly up and down the thread, causing it to twist into strong cotton.

After this process has been completed it is wound into skeins and placed in rice water, which is boiled for many hours, afterwards the skeins of cotton being placed on a bamboo rack and stretched out to dry in the sun, during which process it is combed vigorously with a comb made from the fruit of the screw pine, all stray ends being in this manner separated from the cotton. This process of boiling in rice water is continued several times, and at last these skeins of cotton are placed on a large winding wheel and is wound into balls ready for use.

Indigo dye is made by the pounding of indigo leaves and the boiling of the same, after which the cotton is dipped into the dye and hung up to dry in the sun, this process being repeated many times in order to get a sufficient deepness of colour.

Passing down the village street with the huts ranged on either side, one notices outside most of them a raised bamboo platform where some old

Lakher woman may be seen squatting, sorting her tray full of freshly gathered cotton, placing the good in one heap and the bad in another. The sun being intensely hot she has taken her large cloth and placed it on her head in the form of a large turban. There she sits, wizened with age, with every rib and projecting bone in her body showing distinctly, for it is a rare thing to come upon an aged person in Lakherland who is at all stout, most of the tribesmen being able to boast of being more wiry than having too much superfluous flesh upon their bodies. A little further along we see a young girl seeding her cotton. Another one, maybe, is weaving, and as you pass by you will hear their cheery voices calling out the old familiar phrase, " Na tla chy bao ma ? " which being literally translated means, " Are you at the present-time well ? "

Our next object of interest will be a group of Lakher children playing with their large round beans, very similar to the horse-chestnut, but flattened on both sides and measuring one and a half inches in diameter. These beans go by the name of " Sei-lyu," and are used by both girls and boys to amuse themselves, although the girls are the greater players and exceedingly clever do they become in the manipulation of these curious playthings, placing them in the hollow of the leg behind the knee and ejecting them in such a manner that they go flying through the air knocking other beans which are stood up on end at a distance of some two or three yards. They also place them on their nose, on their elbows, and on every joint in the body, with a clever motion causing them to spin towards their goal. This game is practically the only game amongst children in Lakherland, for there is almost no child-life for these primitive people. As soon as they are able to toddle they learn to carry a basket, the weight of which is added to as time goes on by the addition of a cucumber and so forth, until the child reaches the age of five or six years, when he or she has to start life in real earnest by fetching water and wood or in helping to carry vegetables from the cultivations according to their strength; and the result is, that all the children bear what is known as "The old man look" in their very earliest infancy, and it is our sincere desire that in the coming years the Lakher Pioneer Mission School may be the means of bringing back to Lakherland child-life which is the very essence of home life.

Already great strides have been made towards this end, and the Lakher tribesmen who have entered the Mission School have had to some extent a revival of the spirit of youth which in the coming years we trust, should the Lord spare us, reach out to the very youngest boys and girls of the villages of Lakherland and give to them that joy in life with which God meant that all His creatures should be blessed. This will mean that we must endeavour to obtain the very youngest of the tribes to enter the school to partake in wholesome and child-like games, and this will be made possible only through the co-operation of those in the Homeland who love the children and will band themselves together to help us in this great endeavour which will mean a great uplifting for these primitive tribes. "Suffer the little ones to come unto Me" were the Saviour's words. How much more then should we put forth every effort and every power within our command that the little ones from the age of five and upwards should be gathered in to the Mission School.

Both boys and men are very fond of the pellet and bow, most of the spare time of the boys of the village is spent in roaming the jungle close at hand, and woe betide any little bird which may perch within range of their very effective weapon.

Passing along the village a little further afield we see a man sitting on his verandah plaiting a basket of bamboo, and another plaiting a rain-hat for his wife to wear. The Lakher rain-hats consist of a large round disc a little over two feet in diameter, slightly cancave, the outside being made of very finely-woven cane, ofttimes of most beautiful workmanship. Underneath this is placed a number of leaves, and to keep these in place another cane wicker-work hat with large apertures is plaited, being fastened by cane ties to the outside of the hat very securely, thus keeping the leaves in place. In the centre of the under concave side of this hat is a rim about an inch and a half in depth formed of bamboo, which is made of sufficient size to fit the head of the woman who is to wear it. This rim is fastened very securely to the hat itself, and fixed on to it are two fine cords made from the bark of a tree; these are fastened in a knot under the chin, the Lakher being unable to tie a bow. The brim of the hat is then finished off with three finely-split canes, and when worn by the men or women will protect them, for the greater part, from the rain. The Lakhers, however, have not much objection to their bodies and clothes getting wet, their chief anxiety is to keep their hair and heads dry, and for this purpose this very picturesque rain-hat serves admirably.

Lakher hut with a warrior's wife chopping wood in the foreground (*p.* 135).

Lakher maiden wearing rain hat with bamboo water-pot in her hand (*p.* 140).

[*To face p.* 140.

Standing on the corner of the verandah we espy an old grandmother with her little grand-daughter on her back supported by a large native cloth, which is thrown over one shoulder and under the other, and tied with a knot in the front of the chest. She is smoking her peculiar pipe with the water bowl underneath. Her face and body are extremely filthy, having the dirt of many years upon it, for a Lakher seldom washes after attaining the age of about thirty-five, and before that age indeed their baths consist of a sprinkle of water and a rub down with the hands. The grandchild on her back is under two years of age, and for some reason or another starts up screaming. There being no babies' bottles or comforters in this wild country, the Lakhers have to resort to their own methods, and what is our surprise to find that this old grandmother soon has a comforter close at hand for the little one. She slowly withdraws the pipe from her mouth, and placing the stem of it over her shoulder puts it into the little infant's mouth, who very readily takes a draw at the weed and is immediately soothed, for both men, women and children are all smokers, and their tobacco is obtained from their own gardens, the leaf being plucked at certain seasons of the year and placed in the sun to dry, which causes it to turn almost black. These dry leaves are then rubbed between the palms of the hands and are stored away in bags and hung up in a convenient place in their huts to last them for the year. The pipes of the Lakher men and women are practically the same as those which were described as belonging to the Lushai tribes, the design and decorations only differing.

One of the duties of the women is to supply

nicotine-water for the use of the family, and this is obtained from the vessel, which is half filled with water, at the base of the women's pipes, the nicotine travelling down from the tobacco into the water, and when of sufficient strength is poured into a small calabash gourd.

One of these gourds containing nicotine-water is carried by every Lakher man and woman, and when a young man is courting a maid she supplies him continually with nicotine-water from her pipe for him to carry along in his satchel, which he sips from time to time, and after keeping it in his mouth for a few minutes, will expectorate upon the ground. The Lakhers all claim that without the use of this nicotine-water they are far less able to do their daily work; and it is certainly true that where men have a constant supply of this noxious fluid they appear to work faster and more cheerfully, and I have never been able to discover a case, search as I may, where it appears to harm their health in any way, although the habit in itself is exceedingly objectionable and one which we should dearly love to see banished from amongst the people whose welfare we seek.

Wending our way down the village street we shall probably find two women pounding clay on a flat stone with their pestles, mixing with it a kind of sand, while close at hand we shall see the figure of another wizened old woman sitting on the verandah with her legs straight out holding in her hands a round stone and a wooden mallet covered with thread. With these she is causing the clay to take the form of a pot. The round stone being placed inside a hole in this clay, she keeps up a repeated tapping with the mallet on the outside, and slowly but surely the shape of a very well formed pot appears, which she places very carefully aside, and when she has completed several of these most useful utensils she places them in the sun to dry. When they are thoroughly dried by the rays of the sun, she places them in a heap on the flat ground in front of her hut, and then takes a large quantity of wood, standing it on end round these pots in the form of a cone; and as the sun sinks in the west she places a lighted torch to the bottom of this pile, the wood immediately catching light and burning in the form of a large bonfire for the space of an hour and a half or more.

When the fire is thoroughly burnt out the pots are very carefully removed from the ashes, and when cool are rubbed over both inside and out with some dry leaves the utensils now being ready for use.

The clay of which these pots are made, and also the bowls of the women's pipes, is formed by the white ant, and is not very plentiful in the country, but is gathered in little lots from here and there. Upon this certain clay, also a certain edible mushroom springs up, sometimes once and sometimes twice a year, which is greatly relished by the Lakhers, and which we ourselves have found a very welcome addition to our exceedingly unvaried diet.

As the sun is setting in the west we hear the shrill voices of the housewives calling in their pigs, who know the voices so well and immediately rush out of the jungle and run to their owner, knowing that there is a tasty meal of the bran from rice and boiled leaves awaiting them. This call is a very shrill one and pierces through the air for a great distance, and is caused by a repeated trembling of the tongue in a series of greatly rolled r's thus, "arrrrrr." After this meal the pigs are carefully housed under the hut for the night, or, as more often happens, they object to being fastened up and immediately scamper away again, and as the Lakhers are not very anxious in exerting themselves in regard to their domestic animals, they are allowed their own way.

Night comes on, and rice being plentiful in the village at this season of the year, it is more than likely that we shall find that there is a beer drink being held at one or other of the huts. Those who are invited to this drinking bout assemble on the verandah of the house, where several beer pots made of clay, standing about two feet in height and about a foot and a half in diameter, are arranged, filled to the brim with rice beer which has been brewed at great labour by the women. In the centre of this beer is a long, fine-hole bamboo acting as a straw, which projects to the distance of three or four inches above the surface of the fluid. Another bamboo is also placed in the beer pot, its top reaching about an inch below the surface. By the side of this beer pot, a stool made from the trunk of a tree and cut out in the shape of an hour-glass, is placed, and the men in turn take their seat on this stool and draw the rice beer through the hollow bamboo in the centre. They remain there sipping up the fluid until the top of the bamboo which was below the surface is level with the surface of the beer, when a bamboo water-pot of water is brought and the beer pot is again filled to the top, and the next one in turn sits down on this little stool and repeats the same process, and so throughout the whole circle gathered to the drink, each time the beer pot being filled up to the brim with fresh water, thus as the drinking goes on the beer becomes weaker and weaker, till at last there is very little of the taste of beer in it. It is, however, a very rare thing to find a woman drinking at the beer pot. They have plenty of work in supplying the water and looking after the needs of the men. Now and again only will we find a woman sitting down at the beer pot, although they all love it, yet they are not to be considered as such drinkers of beer as the men are. All night the drinking bout will be kept up, and if it happens to be some special occasion it will continue for three days and three nights without stopping.

The first effect of the beer is to make the men very heated in argument, and the noise of their talking one against the other is tremendous, causing the night air to sound and resound again with their loud voices. The next effect that we notice is that they become very war-like and angry, and it is a common thing for several of them to commence fighting one another with large pieces of wood which were intended for the fire, but being handy find a lodging place across the heads or backs of their opponents.

As the drinking is kept up hour after hour, during the whole time numbers of them are dancing their heathen dances, and being clad only with a small loin cloth, their large knobs of hair on their foreheads, their dark naked bodies and their exceedingly savage attitudes in the weird light of the wood fire which is burning in the hut, make them appear more like a gathering of demons than human beings.

And so the drinking bout is continued, until at last the floor of the verandah is strewn with men thoroughly intoxicated and worn out; the beer having been all consumed the spectacle ceases, and for the next few days none of those who have taken part are able to do anything but sleep until the effects have passed off.

Such is the enjoyment which these primitive savage people find, such is the way in which they live, such is the height of their ambition, without Christ, without hope, seeking to obtain the fill of their enjoyment in this world, and those who know of the Great Love of the Son of God, Who died on Calvary to save these His children, are sitting at home in ease and quietude, not realizing their responsibility in winning them from the very gates of Hell, to decorate as jewels the Crown of the King of Kings.

These are the diamonds in the rough which when cut and burnished by the Great and Everlasting Love of the Son of God shall beam forth with exceeding lustre across the dark wastes and demon-haunted jungles of Lakherland.

How many sheep are straying, lost from the Saviour's fold?
Upon the lonely mountains they shiver with the cold;
Within the tangled thickets, where poisoned vines do creep;
And over rocky ledges wander the poor lost sheep.

Oh, come, let us go and find them,
In the paths of death they roam,
At the close of the day, 'twill be sweet to say—
I have brought some lost one home.

Oh! who will go to find them? who, for the Saviour's sake,
Will search with tireless patience, through briar and thro' brake?
Unheeding thirst or hunger, who still from day to day,
Will seek, as for a treasure, the sheep that are astray?

Say will you seek to find them?—From pleasant bowers
of ease,
Will you go forth determined to find the "least of these"?
For still the Saviour calls them, and looks across the wold,
And still He holds wide open the door into His fold.

How sweet 'twould be at evening, if you and I could
say—
Good Shepherd, we have been seeking the sheep that
went astray,
Heartsore and faint with hunger, we heard them making
moan,
And lo! we come at nightfall and bear them safely
home.

Oh, come, let us go and find them,
In the paths of death they roam,
At the close of the day 'twill be sweet to say—
I have brought some lost one home.

CHAPTER XI

FROM CRADLE TO GRAVE

THE lot of the new-born babe in Lakherland is not in any way to be envied, for it is doomed to go through an ordeal of treatment where it is a case of the "Survival of the Fittest."

The babe is born with very little ceremony under the most primitive and roughest circumstances imaginable, with very little inconvenience to the mother, and will in the usual manner start to cry. During the birth there is practically no privacy, friends and fellow-villagers being present in the hut in large numbers, and the little one from the very first is as a rule not allowed any covering whatever. During the first twenty-four hours the babe may cry a good deal, and it is considered by the Lakher women a sign that the little one is hungry. A pot of rice already cooked is speedily brought and placed before the mother, who takes a handful and chewing it well in her mouth places her mouth against that of the infant and ejects the half-chewed food into the mouth of her new-born babe, and if it finds any difficulty in swallowing this food it is laid gently on its back until the law of gravitation has overcome the difficulty.

Almost every time the little one cries it is supplied with this food, always being fed in this way, which is very similar to the mode of a pigeon with its young. Thus for the first few days this continues, and on the tenth day all Lakher babies pass through a special kind of fever, which determines whether they are strong enough to continue this life.

This fever is brought on entirely through the custom of feeding these young babies on boiled rice, and in a great number of cases the tenth day terminates the existence of the babe. Should, however, the little one have an exceedingly strong constitution, it will overcome this fever and will struggle on through infancy, being carried on its mother's back for the first two years of its childhood and during that time will but in a very slow manner develop. A child of two years of age can say but very few words, and is only just commencing to toddle.

Lakher women on giving birth to a child never go outside of their hut for the first ten or fifteen days, and it will be noticed here how peculiarly this coincides with the law of the Days of Purification given to the Children of Israel, and which the Lakhers call " Naw-khu. . . Tlô."

On the birth of a female child the mother is confined to the hut for ten days, and on the birth of a male child this time is extended to fifteen days, during which period she is not allowed to fetch her wood or her water or to do any of the common duties of the feminine race. The father also, whilst he may go about his daily work, may not cut down any trees or work of that kind, and should necessity call for him to do so he must take a few chips of the tree which he has been cutting home with him and place them by the side of the infant, where they remain throughout these Days of Purification, and the same custom is carried out in reference to certain leaves, a specimen of which must also be placed alongside the infant.

At the end of this period a little ceremony takes place of sprinkling the child with water, and the name which the child is to bear through life is then given to it, while immediately after the father escorts the mother to the outside of her hut, and as soon as this ceremony is over both parents are free to carry on their several duties as usual.

Amongst the Lakhers, in reference to their marriage ceremonies, there is also a system of practically an engagement of marriage which happens previous to the actual marriage ceremony. In the first place one of the peculiarities of the Lakher tribesmen is that they will never approach anybody themselves on any subject, but always speak through a third person. Lakhers, however, do not obtain their wives free, but purchase them with brass gongs, guns, beads and gayal, and ofttimes give very heavy prices for them.

In the first place, when a man desires to marry a woman, he immediately goes to some friend of his and asks him or her to go and speak to her father for him, the girl not being considered. If the father consents to the offer of marriage, the proposed bridegroom takes his "Takô" (chopper) or his spear, and going to the house of his fiancée will stick the Takô or spear in the wall of the hut and depart. The placing of the Takô or spear in this way takes the place of our engagement ring.

He then will serenade his future wife with a Jew's Harp, made of bamboo and string, from night to night, and many are the sweet strains that he will cause this little primitive instrument to send forth. But it will not be long before the proposed husband will be obliged to bring along part of the money for his bride, and when this is done a feast is called and in the usual manner the beer, with the sacrifice of a large pig, is uppermost, the flesh of the pig being much enjoyed by all those called to partake of it.

After this engagement, the man, who may belong to a village some few days' journey away, will return for many months or even for many years. When he is ready, however, to take his wife he will bring another large portion of the marriage price along with a number of pigs, for at the wedding ceremony the bridegroom is obliged to kill half the number of pigs that the bride's father or elder brother may choose to slaughter. Thus if the bride's brother should decide to kill five pigs, which is practically the lowest number he is allowed to kill, the bridegroom has to supply three more, making eight pigs slaughtered for the feast; but in many cases the bride's brother will kill as many as ten pigs, and with the bridegroom's five will give a feast of fifteen pigs, which have all to be eaten during the ceremony, that lasts for a number of days and nights consecutively.

During this ceremony the bridegroom takes his wife, and from this time forth they live together; but at this period the whole of the marriage price has not been given, for it is so great that no Lakher can afford to pay for it right off, but it extends throughout the whole of his lifetime, and should he have been unable to pay the whole amount during his life, the burden of his wife's price falls on his eldest son, and if not paid during that generation, it again falls on his grandson, so ofttimes the price of the bride is handed down for several generations, causing each one to be in debt with the other, and an exceedingly hard thing it is for a Lakher to be free from liabilities in this respect.

The father of the bride receives very little of the money if there is an elder son, the eldest son always receiving the price of his sisters. This price, payable to the bride's eldest brother, consists of no less than thirteen sections, each section having a name and varying in its amount accordingly. Out of these thirteen sections the father receives three of the smaller sums, while two other sections are paid to the friend of the father of the bride and to the bride's uncle. Besides these amounts mentioned, there are still nine more sections, each bearing its own name, payable to the bride's mother's brother (Bride's Uncle), whilst he passes along two of these smaller sections, one to his best friend, and one to the bride's grandmother's brother on the mother's side (Bride's Great Uncle). At the death of a wife a heavy death due has to be paid to the dead wife's eldest brother, and the death due upon a woman is heavier than that upon a man, while the death due upon a prosperous person is heavier than that upon a poor person.

The marriage prices given for the bride are so exceedingly complicated that one can easily see that without careful study and thought it would be impossible for one to understand them fully, and for this reason we do not propose to weary our reader with more of these knotty problems. Suffice it to say that the ordinary people in Lakher give to the value of about £10 4*s.* 8*d.* for their bride, whilst one of the ruling clan will give as much as £44 14*s.* 8*d.*, and at the death of the wife a death due of about £1 6*s.* 8*d.* and £10 respectively will have to be paid. These sums, it will be easily understood, are exceedingly heavy for the people who have to meet them. Why the bride's uncle should be able to claim on the marriage of his nieces is a matter which it would be hard to fathom out.

While the marriage feast is proceeding and a satisfactory part of the price has been paid—for there will be no sign of the bride until that is forthcoming—the bride is seen escorted by a large band of men and girls, proceeding from the house in which she has been staying, to the house where the feast is being held, marching in Indian file with all their arms folded and in perfect silence. On her arrival she is the man's wife and in due course goes back to his village with him, but during the first part of their married life they as a rule live in the bridegroom's parents' home, and after children are born they generally take to their own abode.

A Lakher may become engaged at almost any age: it entirely depends upon whether he can afford to pay the preliminary price for his bride or not. If he can do so, he may become engaged as early as eight years of age, and the preliminary feastings and ceremonies will be gone through, after which he will retire to his village until he is mature, for the Lakhers never allow matrimony until the age of maturity is reached; and it is a noticeable thing throughout the country that their families are not in any way large as a rule, considering the number of inhabitants in a village the number of children will be found to be comparatively small, whilst amongst some of the neighbouring tribes the number of children in the villages will be found to be large in comparison.

Whilst amongst the Lakhers divorce is easy, there are very few cases of the same. On the other hand, a man is allowed as many wives as he can afford to pay for. "Thylai," Chief of Sherkor, for instance, can count up to seven wives—his powers of reckoning seem to fail him beyond, although there are probably many more; but in all cases where more than one wife is kept they always live in separate huts, and as a rule in separate villages, each being visited in turn from time to time.

On the other hand, a wife may only have one husband, and the Lakhers throughout the whole of their tribes, while winking at the non-virtue of their maidens, hold with abhorrence any act of adultery. This, however, is only on the feminine side, a man being practically free from blame.

While the laws of the tribes allow a man to have many wives, yet but one woman is held as his legitimate bride, all the others being termed concubines, and the offsprings of these latter are counted unworthy to cook the food at their sacrificial ceremonies, the cooking of which is deemed a great honour.

According to Lakher custom, the young men of the village never sleep in their own homes, but every night as darkness sets in they will go to some neighbour's hut as they feel disposed, and there will they sleep until the morning, whilst the maidens of the village never leave their home. This custom does not lean towards virtue, both men and women sleeping side by side on the floor of the hut, yet with all this it is surprising to find the high moral tone of the Lakhers at large, the greater number of their maidens remaining virtuous, and it is surprising to find, when considering the conditions of life, how few infants are born out of wedlock, and even when this is so, a marriage as a rule takes place.

In any case a heavy fine is inflicted approximate to the value of £2 13*s.* 4*d.*, which would be paid in gongs or kind for the transgression.

With all these customs, however, the Lakhers have a code of just laws, and throughout the whole tribes their vices are very few, the greatest being perhaps that of drink. Their morals run high, and there is great hope that with the advent of Christianity amongst them they may speedily become a highly moral race of men and women which will be an honour to Christendom at large.

As soon as a Lakher dies, if he is the owner of a gun, or if the family can borrow a gun for the time being from any of their fellow-villagers, a shot is fired, and sometimes two or three, into the air from the outside of the hut, and with all speed a " Wake " is called for.

During the time that the deceased has been lying at death's door his house has been filled with relatives and friends who have whiled away the hours drinking rice beer, and immediately life has left the body and the shot has been fired, the huge brass gongs which almost every Lakher possesses are brought into play, and these boom out the doleful knell of the dead.

The women immediately set to work to procure all the beer they can, and every beer pot is brought into use, being filled to the brim with the sweet fluid, and the " Wake " commences, whilst the very near relatives set to work taking the dead person and placing him or her on a kind of stretcher made of two bamboo poles and a cloth in a similar way to which we make a stretcher in first aid to the injured.

This stretcher is placed in a diagonal position against the wall, and the corpse is placed on the stretcher dressed in all its best robes and decorated with all the beads that the deceased possessed in life, along with any other ornaments; and if he is the possessor of a plume, the plume also is placed in his hair.

Before this stretcher the wife and daughters kneel, chanting their heathen chants and every few minutes rending the air with a heart-rending shriek, bowing themselves before the corpse with their heads covered with their white cloth, lamenting the dead, whilst all around inside and outside of the hut the relatives and friends gather round the beer pots talking one against the other, chanting their heathen chants and beer songs, laughing and joking, and as time goes on quarrelling and fighting, while the whole of the time the wife and daughters or the very nearest of kin wail in a most heart-rending manner, and these cries and yells pass through one as a cry of a lost soul, for they have died without hope, with everything before them unpierceable darkness, with every fear of the evil spirits wreaking their vengeance on them to the utmost.

This will continue for many days, sometimes as long as five, until the corpse gives forth such offensive odours that it is impossible for it to remain longer, and these odours can be realized ofttimes at some great distance from the hut itself.

During the "Wake" one of the near relatives is allotted off to dig the grave, and very little help he will get from any of those gathered together in the hut, and as they are having what they term a good time he too sees no reason why he shouldn't join them every now and again for some long period, and thus the digging of the grave proceeds very slowly, thus causing them to keep the dead body in the hut longer than otherwise would be the case, for the Lakhers are very unkind towards one another in this respect. They hardly know what it is to help one another in a time of need, or at least they are very reluctant to do so, but one thing we have been bound to notice, that where Lakher tribesmen have entered our school, where they are taught to do all they can for one another; we have found them putting aside their own leisure time to help some villager in the grave-digging when there has been no pressure or persuasion brought to bear upon them, thus showing the effect of Christian influence which has been brought to bear upon them in their school training.

The mode of grave-digging amongst the Lakhers differs to some extent from the mode exercised by the surrounding tribes. They first of all mark a square of four feet on the ground and start digging and continue until they have dug to a depth of about three feet. This gives them sufficient room in which to swing their native implements. When they have thoroughly cleaned out this pit they commence on one side to burrow out a hole two feet in diameter in a slightly vertical position, and thus they continue to do until they have bored down a distance of about six feet. This burrow they very carefully clear of all loose earth, and when this is completed the grave is ready to receive the corpse.

The family next commence to prepare the dead for the burial, which takes them some little time.

The dead man's spirit cannot be allowed to traverse to the "A Thi-pa Khi" by itself, and therefore some domestic animal must be sacrificed in order that the spirit of this animal may accompany him on his journey into the after-world. As a rule the animal is a dog, which is strangled by means of a noose around its neck suspended high up in the air on a pole outside the hut of the deceased, this animal often dying in great agony. After its death it is cut down and the friends gathered in the hut place it in a pot of boiling water, after singeing the hair off the body, boil it for their feast, the flesh of which they much relish.

After this sacrifice has been completed the dead man is placed in his best cloth, which entirely covers him head and feet, so that no part of the body is visible, but before this is done the greater part of his ornaments are taken from him and are kept as heirlooms.

As the sun sinks in the west a small procession may be seen coming out of the hut, the foreman carrying the rifle, and as soon as they are outside he will fire a couple of shots into the air, while two men, one at the feet and the other at the head, carry the dead man to the grave. They place him carefully in the pit, then taking him feet first push him down into the burrow, and with a large slab of stone completely shut up the entrance.

As soon as this is done, one or two of them commence filling in the pit with earth, erecting a large post some ten or twelve feet in length which they have previously prepared and carved out in fantastic shapes (and at times the ornamentations on these posts are very cleverly cut), place the end of it in the pit and tamp down the earth firmly around it, this post being the monument to the deceased person. The outer margin of this pit is then marked out in stones and forms a permanent tomb to the dead man.

In the course of a few days the family will hang a

small wicker basket on the monumental post and place in it various fruits, for the greater part consisting of bananas, while the skull of the animal sacrificed at the time of the man's death will be securely fastened to the post above it. This fruit is placed there for the express purpose of feeding the spirit, and of saving any evil spirit from entering into the house of the deceased.

At the close of a year after the burial a very interesting ceremony is carried out, which goes by the name of "Ra-kha . . . tla," the idea of which is to cause the spirit of the departed man never to return again to his hut, for it is believed at times that he comes and sits upon his tombstone, a matter which the Lakhers greatly dread.

This ceremony consists of a dance, when all in the family gather together with friends and in the usual manner have a large beer-drinking bout, while outside on the little piece of flat ground in the front of the hut are ten bamboos arranged parallel to one another, at the ends of which sit five small boys of the village with the end of a bamboo in each hand, and then in time, to the beat of the drums and the playing of cymbals, these boys hit the bamboos on a log of wood which is placed crossways at either end, lifting them again into the air they bring each two bamboos into contact with each other, making a very fascinating noise, keeping time the whole while, whilst the young men and maidens of the family, dressed in their best apparel and carrying the gun of the deceased and wearing his many ornaments, dance in a most clever way between these bamboos as they are being worked by the boys, hardly ever making a mis-step.

At this time a pig is generally killed, which forms

the chief part of the feast, and the whole ceremony is completed within the twenty-four hours.

If the deceased happened to be a very influential man, at this time a monument of stones is raised to him at some suitable spot outside the village, and his relations are very particular to see that everything in regard to all these ceremonies is carried out to the letter.

It is an interesting fact that in the monuments to the dead there is a difference between the monument raised to a man and the monument raised to a woman, which varies in different villages to some slight extent, but the most general way of discerning to which sex the dead person belonged is by looking at the monument towards the top; for in the case of a man the sides of this monument are as a rule parallel with an ornamented square at the top representing a head, but in the case of one erected to a woman, just below this head on either side of the post will be noticed two large nitches chopped out, which causes the design to look as if it has a waist.

When an infant dies these same ceremonies do not take place, for an infant is always placed in an earthenware pot which forms its coffin, and a little water is placed into this pot along with it, and it is as a rule buried away in the jungle. This difference will be accounted for by their belief about the spirit of an infant being looked after by God as before referred to.

There is another mode of burial which is sometimes practised for chiefs. The pit of the grave is dug in the usual way, but instead of a burrow only being made, the burrow leads into a little underground chamber and the body of the dead is placed in a recumbent position on the floor of this chamber. In such a case as this, however, the ornaments are placed with the dead man and left there until the next member of the family dies, when the grave is re-opened and the lately deceased is laid alongside the body already there, whilst the ornaments of the first buried are then removed and kept in the family as heirlooms.

In regard to the first mode of burial, this grave is often re-opened for the next deceased of the family, if the body which was first buried has had time to decay. The burrow being dug vertically the bones will naturally fall down to the further end of the burrow, and will leave room for the new burial.

The Lakhers do not always bury their dead outside their own houses. At times they do, but at other times they will make their graves outside of some neighbour's house, believing that if the grave is not outside the hut of the deceased the spirit will not enter into the hut and do harm to the family; but should the grave be outside the deceased's hut the spirit is liable to enter in and wreak vengeance for some matter that has not been carried out to the letter.

The Lakhers also have a mode on certain occasions of building a small hut over the grave of the newly buried, in which they will place various fruits for the spirit to feed upon, but as soon as these huts fall to pieces a sacrifice is undertaken and a monumental post is erected and the grave banked up with huge stones, preferably fetched from some place which they hold sacred.

CHAPTER XII

WAR TACTICS AND FOLKLORE

THE Lakhers were until within the last few years a notorious head-hunting race of wild hillsmen, delighting not only in the chase of wild animals but in the chase for human beings, raiding and pillaging any villages that they might come across when on the war-path.

Not only was this head-hunting carried on against neighbouring tribes but greatly amongst themselves, one village against another, ofttimes situated only twelve or twenty miles apart. During the rainy season raiding was practically unknown, the people being full of work on their cultivations would for the greater part spend their time in attending to their year's supplies, but no sooner had the dry season set in than large numbers of these people would gather together at a great feast and decide in which direction they should seek for heads and slaves.

Ofttimes several villages would club together and form one party about a thousand strong, and with the usual feasting and slaughter of many pigs, while the drinking of beer was always uppermost, they would practise their warlike dances and spend their time in speculating on the sport that lay ahead of them.

One of the most curious customs of these Lakhers

when about to go on a raid was concerned with the beer pot. They made a syphon of two bamboos joined in the form of an angle by a brass head-piece very fantastically decorated. The one end of this syphon they placed in the beer pot in an upright position, while the other naturally fell outside of the beer pot and terminated very near to the ground. One of the warriors then stretched himself out on the ground and placed his mouth to the end of this syphon, sucking at it and causing the beer to flow of its own account into a small bamboo trough or bowl placed to receive it, after which he would join his fellows and the whole of the party very attentively listened to the beer passing through the syphon. If the beer flowed in a smooth, steady course with no sound within the tube, then the raid was considered to be blessed, and come what may would be carried into force. Should, however, the beer start to make a gurgling sound in the syphon they believed that it was a sure sign that should they go on this particular raid they themselves would be the conquered and not the conquerors, and therefore the whole raid would be abandoned, so that upon this very small matter was the issue of war or peace.

All the Lakher tribes are so deep in the feudal system that to keep peace between them is a very difficult matter. At the present time, however, Government being so near at hand, the influence of mission work having taken so strong a hold amongst them, feudal warfare will, in a few years we hope, become a thing of the past. Even the very nearest of kin would raid one another, and each village had to keep a strict watch over their country and village in order not to be taken by surprise.

At the distance of about a mile from the village fortifications used to be built, which were generally formed by the felling of a great number of large trees, of the cutting of a large belt of bamboos so placed that the sharp ends of these made an exceedingly formidable barrier. At certain points in this fortification viaducts were made, and by the side of these viaducts a small hut erected, where two Lakher warriors were always on watch for the enemy, being relieved at certain periods by another couple of their tribesmen. Immediately the sign of an approaching enemy was indicated, one of these warriors would bear the news to the village with all speed, while the other would keep watch to ascertain the movements of the enemy.

The Lakher villages are built on the hill tops, and for the greater part are built along the crests of precipices, with perhaps only one path by which the village can be entered. In the centre of the village or close at hand an extra fortification was made in the shape of a "Block-house," called by them a "Ku," which was constructed on a similar plan to our castles surrounded by a moat with a drawbridge of feudal times.

The "Ku" consisted of a large plot of ground walled round by the upright trunks of small trees, the ends being buried firmly in the ground and rising to a height of eight or ten feet, placed side by side and ofttimes two or three deep, making a practically impenetrable wall for bullets from the enemy's flint-lock guns, whilst this wall had in certain places small divisions left in order that the refugees within could fire upon the enemy without, and watch their movements in comparative safety. On the outside of this wall a large trench was dug about eight feet in breadth and six feet deep. At the bottom of this trench were placed short, sharpened bamboos which made it impossible for the native with bare feet to get across. The back side of this castle was protected by a huge precipice, so that the enemy could never approach in the rear. A drawbridge of planks formed the entrance to the castle, and after the children, women and men had all retreated to their place of refuge, these planks were drawn up, thus leaving a formidable task before the enemy.

Lakhers, however, in all their raids never besieged a village ; a few hours and all was past. Should they gain the village, however, and find the people gone, as far as it was possible they would pillage every home, carrying off with them everything of value. Where possible, they would seize their enemy alive in preference to killing him, and from henceforth he or she would become their slave and would be taken back to their village to live a life of slavery and contempt. If, however, capture was out of the question, the person was speedily decapitated and the head carried to the village as a token of the warrior's bravery.

Should a captive slave endeavour to escape he was immediately hunted down and brought back to the village, when a large log of wood about four feet in length, having a hole sufficiently big in the centre to insert the foot, and which was known as a "Kei-hrai," was procured, and the unfortunate slave was made to place his foot in this hole, after which an iron pin was driven from one side of the log to the other, passing through the orifice close above the heel of the slave, thus making it impossible for him to withdraw his foot from the stock.

A rope was then fastened from one end of the log to the other sufficiently long enough to just pass over his shoulder, and when wishing to move, by means of this rope the heavy stock had to be lifted from off the ground and in this way he was enabled to shuffle along, an ordeal which inflicted much torture.

The Lakhers, however, did not care for carrying away young men and women to any great extent, as they gave them far too much trouble, but could they manage to seize the younger children they never missed the opportunity, as the child was not so liable to find his way back through the jungle and in a very short space of time would forget his parents, his village and his tribe, and thus become speedily reconciled.

The Lakhers have two kinds of slaves, those made captives in war and those made slaves from amongst their own villagers, for the greater part in lieu of payment of debt, and also the offsprings of these slaves; and one of the greatest objections to slavery amongst the Lakhers is the fact that the owner of a female slave will give her away in marriage without receiving but a very small marriage price, realizing that all the offsprings that may be the result increase the number of his slaves and therefore increase his wealth.

Lakherland, consisting for the greater part of huge precipices and steep inclines, forcing an entrance into the various villages was an exceedingly difficult undertaking, and in order to stop the attacking party from approaching further, the Lakhers at certain points of the road high up on the hillside, built large stone shoots which consisted of a firm platform built in such a position as to overhang the brow of the hill, supported on either side by the trunks of friendly trees. Upon this platform huge boulders used to be rolled, and stones of various sizes heaped up, whilst the platform was made in such a manner that the cutting through of one or two canes or bamboos would sufficiently weaken it to cause the weight of the stones to break it down.

These shoots remained in readiness for the enemy, and as soon as warning was given of the approach of the raiding party members of the tribe would hurry to the stone shoots and as the advancing party passed below on the hillside, with their *takôs* would cut these canes and bamboos through and the whole mass of stones would crash down upon the invading party, causing great havoc and slaughter, and ofttimes to such an extent that a further advance of the enemy was retarded. The dead would then be decapitated and carried off to the village with great rejoicing.

There is a particular kind of earth that resembles pipe-clay in consistency, but is slightly harder and of a greyish nature, which the Lakhers often eat and claim for it the power of sustaining a man for thirty-six hours or more when food is not procurable and when subjected to great privation. Especially is this peculiar kind of earth sought after by Lakher women in the state of expectant motherhood. This earth, however, does not lie on the surface of the ground, but may be found under the ground in certain spots in large lumps with the appearance of rocks.

Let us turn our attention to a few items of interest in the folklore of these people, and as in every nation of the world there is a record of the Deluge in their ancient history, so amongst the Lakher tribes we find one of interest, and let us quote the history in e manner and way in which the people know of it.

"In the beginning God (Kha-zo-pa) made the sea and land (note here the reference to one God). The land had running through it a great number of rivers, whilst in the middle of this land was the sea. At the bottom of this was a large hole through which the sea continually flowed, thus clearing away the waters that came from the rivers, and itself not becoming of increased size.

"God next made the prawn and the crab and placed them in the sea and gave them a particular work to do, which consisted of keeping this hole at the bottom of the sea clear of all rubbish, so as to allow a free exit to the flow of the sea water. This hole naturally caused a whirlpool, but the prawn worked so hard at clearing the rubbish away from the bottom of this vortex that its claws wore down until greatly reduced in size and caused it to be unable to fulfil the work for which God had made it. The rivers bringing down such quantities of débris from their upper reaches soon filled up this hole, thus the whirlpool became a thing of the past and the sea rapidly started to rise, and not being able to find an exit the waters soon commenced to cover the earth, and men, women and children and all the animals were driven to the top of the highest mountain. At this time human beings and wild animals were in a friendly state, neither of them doing damage to each other.

"The whole of this trouble was brought about by the presence of the devil in the waters of the sea, who made it impossible for anything further to be accomplished by the prawn and the crab, and from the rising waters was heard to issue the word

'Ngai-tai!— — Ngai-tai!— —'

"Now 'Ngai-tai' was a young virgin with an exceedingly beautiful face, in fact the most beautiful person on earth, and she lived with her mother amongst the small band of men, women and children who had been driven by the rising water up to the top of this high mountain.

"The Chief ruling over all these people, when hearing continually 'Ngai-tai' being uttered from the waters, and seeing the continual rise of the same, proclaimed before the people the fact that if this beautiful lass was not thrown into the rising waters the devil would kill all those that were alive by drowning.

"At first the people were loath to make this human sacrifice, and so in the hopes of appeasing the devil they plucked one hair from Ngai-tai's head and threw it into the water, and immediately the water started to subside a little, but only a little, for the hair alone was not sufficient. Then, as a last resort, they took the beautiful virgin and cast her headlong into the waters, and after disappearing for a while she reappeared again and was carried away from them as the water subsided, and her mother weeping bitterly followed after her.

"As the tears rolled down the mother's cheeks she continually wiped them away with the back of her hand, and these being very profuse, the mother in turn wiped the back of her hand against the bamboos which grew along her road; and because of this action of the mother you can take the young bamboos and after putting them in the sun for a month to dry and then burning them with fire, the ashes can be eaten in the place of salt, being the salt from the tears of Ngai-tai's mother.

"While following her daughter she continually carried on a conversation with her, but when the waters had subsided as far as the 'Matu' (Arakan) country, seeing that every hope of ever receiving her daughter back to her again was futile, she commanded her daughter to cause the waters to become salt, and through the action of her daughter the waters of the sea became salt.

"The mother then in great grief and with a longing for revenge returned up country to a village of the name of 'Hna-hro,' and there she caused a stream which gushed from a rock to issue salt water in the place of fresh. This stream remains there to this day and from it the Lakhers obtain their salt, going through the tedious labour of boiling down this water in great quantities and after much fatigue obtaining the sediment which is left and which is salt.

"Thus the flood passed away from off the face of the earth, mankind and beast all living together in perfect friendship, when upon one occasion a mother being out with her little baby met a centipede to whom she spoke, asking a favour of it, who in return nipped her baby and speedily caused its death.

"After this, man said that the animals must depart from amongst them, but they pleaded so hard not to be separated that man forgave them and let them remain.

"Soon after this, however, a boy was making a bow and arrow for himself when a deer (Sa-suh) asked him what he was busy making, in answer to which question the boy informed the deer that

Group of Lakher young women and maidens (*p.* 129).

Lakher men carrying a beer-pot preparing for a festival (*p.* 144).

[*To face p.* 170.

he was making something to kill things with. 'Is that so!' said the deer, 'Well, try it on me and see if it is all right.' So the boy accordingly agreed, and placing his arrow in the string he let it fly, with the result that the deer rolled over dead.

"After this God (Kha-zo-pa) commanded that men and animals must separate and not dwell together, and He caused them to be put asunder, for the centipede had killed the baby and the boy had killed the deer, so from henceforth they must live apart and fight their individual battles themselves."

There is a species of flying lizard in the country which is known as the "Pa-chi-cha-ria-pa." This animal frequents five or six different species of trees as a rule, and is always found in a position with its face turned upwards, while it continually causes its throat to swell in and out in a motion towards the sky. This animal's spirit, in response to the motion of its throat, is believed by the Lakhers to be probing at the son of God (Kha-zo-pa) (notice here the belief in the Son of God), and this continual probing is resented by God's son, who in return sends down upon the animal heavy rain which is disturbed by thunder, and directly at the animal itself thunderbolts are hurled, the thunderbolts striking the tree and either snapping it in two or in other cases peeling the bark from off the trunk, and the animal is either killed or manages to fly away.

The trees on which this animal is found are exceedingly subject to being struck with lightning, and for this reason are never used in the building of huts by the Lakhers, the wood being too great a lightning conductor.

The Lakhers state that these thunderbolts fall to

the earth and bury themselves in the ground, but after three years they come to the surface of their own accord and can be found there.

The origin of thunder as believed by the Lakhers is also interesting.

The python, which is the largest snake in the country and the only one that is considered non-poisonous by the people, grows to an enormous size, and it is believed that when a python has grown to the extent of reaching twelve to sixteen inches in diameter through its body it visits a river, and there in the midst of the stream stands on the end of its tail. If the waters of the river cannot remove it from this position the python says, "Now I am strong enough to go to heaven, but I must first of all try my strength, on a high hill, against the wind."

It immediately makes its way up to the top of the highest mountain and there stands in the same position on its tail till God sends a mighty wind. but with all its force the python is able to withstand it. This being the case, God receives it up to heaven. It has no sooner arrived in heaven than it is overjoyed at the thought, and vehemently beats its tail up and down on the floor of heaven, and this beating of the tail is what we call thunder. (It is worth noting here that the python's spirit is not only received into heaven but its body also, and there is even work for a python there to remind those left on earth of the possibilities of reaching that heaven-land.)

On one occasion it was my fortune to shoot an eagle which measured five feet ten inches from tip to tip of its wings. At another time I shot at one almost as large, the bullet making a small wound on the joint of one wing, causing it to fall to earth, and I was able to procure it alive, while on the next day it was in perfect health and had I given it the opportunity would have flown away with thankfulness. But it was my intention to try and tame the savage bird, which, however, proved fruitless, and after keeping it for several days it started to mope very seriously.

Now the Lakhers have in their folklore the following useful information. "At one time God (Kha-zo-pa) made a water hole purposely for the eagles to drink at, but after executing this kindness the eagles absolutely refused to partake of God's benefits and God in return cursed the water and told them that if they ever drank water at any time they should speedily die, so eagles never partake of the refreshing fluid."

This eagle which I was taming, moping seriously, appeared to me to be in need of water, and although I was well aware of this little piece of folklore I determined to give the bird a drink. Taking a teaspoon and dipping it into a cup of water I emptied the contents of this one teaspoon down its throat. The bird's eyes immediately glared as if overjoyed at having received this drink, but in less than two minutes he was as drunk as could be, reeling from side to side and at last falling down helpless upon the ground. In an hour's time he recovered himself a little and in another half hour he lay dead—proving the accuracy of the chief points in this folklore, and the people tell me that sometimes these eagles may be found lying dead on the rivers' banks, or if not dead, when seen by the side of a river can easily be caught alive, but very shortly after they pass away.

The Lakhers believe that the earth is flat and

that the sky above almost touches the earth at the horizon, whilst the stars and the moon are lamps suspended from the sky.

Where the sky almost meets the earth are a number of cords, and through this space nothing but the swallow and the martin can fly. These two birds alone are able, with the exception of spirits, to pass these cords, as the cords continue to keep up a chopping motion between themselves, and anything attempting to pass them would be immediately hit and killed.

When a chief dies it is believed that the spirit of the chief takes its "Takô" and passing between these cords cuts one or more asunder. This immediately causes the earth to quiver. Thus when in that country we experience an earthquake, which we are often prone to do, the Lakhers believe that a chief has passed away and it is the severing of one of these cords that has caused the earth to quake, and whether, at that time, in their hut or in the street or out in the jungle, immediately they feel the shock you can hear them cry from all points of the compass "I tla ne!" "I tla ne!" meaning "I am well!" "I am well!" believing that by this expression they will escape any harm from the earthquake.

The country boasts of the "Bulbul" bird, referring to which there is interesting folklore.

"A long time ago the domestic fowl had a bunch of red feathers underneath its tail, and the fowls while scratching for their food in the jungle were continually being carried off by eagles, seeming never to know when these birds were about. The Bulbul bird one day approached the fowls on the matter and made a bargain with them, that they should give up their bunch of red feathers for good and allow the Bulbul always to wear them, and in exchange for this sacrifice the Bulbul agreed in its turn always to call out when an eagle was in the vicinity, thus giving the fowls time to run under cover."

Whenever you hear the Bulbul, which is known as the "Phia-bi-pa," screaming out its little shrill note, you will see the domestic fowls without hesitation scamper in all directions to find cover, and in all cases from my own observation I have found that an eagle has been present. The Bulbul is a little bird with this red tuft of feathers under its tail.

With folklore referring to the dog and goat let us end this chapter.

"A long time ago the dog had horns. One day on prowling round the village the dog espied some cleaned rice at the bottom of a mortar outside a Lakher hut, and tried for some time in vain to lick it up, its horns every time preventing its head from getting deep enough into the mortar. After thinking the matter carefully over the dog removed its horns and placed them on the verandah, going back again to the mortar for its longed for repast.

"Now at this time the goat was without horns and lived in the jungle, but happening at this moment to pass by and seeing the dog lay down its horns, thought how nice and useful they would be for its own utilisation, so quietly going over to the verandah the goat placed the horns on its head and with a bound disappeared into the jungle. Since that time dogs have been without horns and goats have been horned animals.

"The dog naturally was very savage at the idea of losing its horns, but it had no possible chance of ever procuring them again, and so whenever a goat came within sight the dog would chase it in anger."

Wherever you find a goat in the country you will find that the native curs are exceedingly savage towards it and often hunt the poor animal very severely, and where it cannot get the goat to run away, it spends a great deal of its time in barking furiously at it.

And so throughout all the folklore of the country in the main points there is a great deal of truth and information which as a Missionary I have found most useful in reaching the hearts of the people. A thorough knowledge of the folklore of the country, with their manners and customs, is one of the surest grounds on which to gain a listening amongst these savage tribes, and ofttimes through knowledge of this sort one is able to give forth the truth which is in Christ Jesus with far more intelligible interest to the people concerned than would be possible were the common knowledge of their own every-day beliefs not understood.

CHAPTER XIII

RAIN AND THE TRAPPER

IN the Lakher country the year is divided into only two seasons, which may be termed the Dry and Rainy Seasons, or the Cold Season and the Rains. When speaking of the cold season it does not of necessity mean that in Lakherland one experiences cold weather, but that it is only cold in contrast to the other part of the year which is extremely hot, namely, during the rains, the thermometer seldom falling below 56° Fahrenheit, and only once during our sojourn in that lonely land did the thermometer fall to 50° for a period of three days and this proved so intensely cold in contrast with the weather generally experienced that a "Slow Paced Loris," which it was our pleasure to have as a pet, died simply from the sudden change of temperature.

This weird-looking animal first of all showed its displeasure in this sudden change by crawling very slowly over its perches, swinging from one to the other and the whole of the time uttering an uncanny snarl. The following day it seemed to have lost a great deal of its strength, and instead of walking in an upright position over its perches, it was obliged to hang to them and walk in a hand over hand manner ; and although we took it out of its cage and placed it in a basket amongst flannel in a convenient spot near the fire, the poor little creature expired on the third day. With its large round eyes staring at one in a most distressing manner, it became intensely savage, so that it was impossible to get near to it. This weird creature, which in life appeared to have no tail, after death we discovered that it had a tail about half an inch in length. It is called by the Lakhers "Ru-lei-pa," which translated means the animal "without bones." This snap of cold was quite an exception, but needless to say the stranger in the country finds the cold weather the most bearable time for travelling from village to village, and one is very glad to have a fire in the evenings.

The cold season sets in practically at the beginning of October, and as we near Christmas the temperature gradually decreases, whilst the month of January is the coldest month of the year. During February and March the sun alters his position, and the days commence to get longer and hotter. April is the month of heavy gales, which come as regularly as clockwork, and each storm has a special name in the native tongue. During this month one experiences six of these hurricanes, ushering in the commencement of the North-West Monsoon.

In the early days of our pioneering, only five months after the completion of the Mission station, we experienced an exceedingly heavy storm which will give one a fair idea of the anxious time which one is bound to experience throughout the month of April. Referring to a letter written home at the time, I find the following graphic description :—

"We have been having some terrific storms of

late, six in all, but the one which we experienced the other afternoon was perhaps the worst. Across the Kolodyne valley, opposite to where our bungalow is situated, there is a high peak of the Paitha Range, probably a distance of six miles as the crow flies from our bungalow. Suddenly we noticed that this peak was capped by a very dark cloud and have now learned from experience that no sooner is this discernible than we have barely time to close every window in the bungalow and make the doors secure ere the storm with all its force and fury bursts upon us.

"On this afternoon we espied the black cap on the mountain peak, and with all speed closed the windows and doors as securely as possible. The storm burst upon us with all its fury, and the whole house seemed to give against the terrific force of the mighty wind, very little rain falling at the commencement, and we were in great fear that the bungalow and all would be swept away. Catching the slender bamboo shutters which closed the aperture in our bungalow where glass should be, but which we had been unable to obtain owing to the expense, it tore one of them open, with the result that before we could do anything the pictures hanging on the walls were soon flying through the air to the floor, and a steel cabin trunk, which was packed full of clothes and was standing close to the window, was moved from its place across the floor.

"In trying to close the window shutter once again the wind caught it and slammed it with such violence that it nearly broke my arm.

"The cook-house at the back of our bungalow is situated nearly fifty feet away, but between it and our house, towards the right hand side, stands an exceedingly large chestnut-tree somewhat over two feet in diameter and of proportionate height. The hurricane catching a huge bough which overhung the pathway between the bungalow and the cook-house snapped it like a twig, and it came crashing down right across the path, and had any one been outside at the time it must have killed them on the spot. Another large tree in the front of our bungalow close at hand, of similar size, was snapped in two, half way up the trunk, and came crashing down, mercifully however parallel with the bungalow.

"The English flag, flying at the masthead in the front garden, was ripped to ribbons, but the Union Jack, that was flying there also, withstood the storm.

"On the verandah in front of the bungalow was standing our large heavy table, some six by four feet in size. The wind in some way or other first knocked it over on its side, and the next gust of wind tore the board top from off the framework, which was nailed on with 2½ inch French nails, and the table lay in different directions ripped to pieces, but with only one board (for it had been made from our packing cases) that was in any way split, so clean and even had been the pressure of the wind. A Tate sugar box, which had contained some of our goods and which we had only recently unpacked, was standing near to the table. The wind which pulled the table to pieces burst open the front door of the bungalow, and stepping out on the verandah to drag the door back into position, I was met with another gust of wind which caught the empty Tate sugar box and carried it several feet off the ground right along the verandah, just missing my head.

"A large fowl-run, which it had taken hours and days to construct of bamboo lattice, was levelled to the ground in a minute, but our fowl-house stood the rage of the storm. A most peculiar thing happened: The fowl-run fence was blown down to the ground, and after a little while the wind changed its direction, raising the fence once again from off the ground and standing it upright, but it was so badly damaged that it was of no use, and we were obliged to take it to pieces and use it for fencing round the garden.

"A camp-bed which happened to be open on the verandah at the time was doing its best to win the £2,000 *Daily Mail* prize for flying between London and Manchester in a heavier than air machine, and it performed the aeroplane feat well along our verandah. A little of this kind of wind bottled up and carried on an aeroplane would soon cause the fortunate owner to win the £2,000 prize.

"There is many a tree, both small and large, torn up and lying on the ground, and bamboos without number snapped, but we are thankful to say that our first bamboo-built house stood it well, and with the exception of a little piece of bamboo being broken on the verandah, no other damage was done; but during the whole of that storm we lived in great fear that any moment we might find ourselves roofless. As soon as the rain deluged down, the wind lost a great deal of its power, for which we were very thankful.

"Down the village there were other scenes. Three of the native huts were levelled with the ground, practically smashed to atoms, while a fourth was robbed of its roof and which lay as a mass of débris in the jungle at some little distance. A small bamboo house just below our compound was all but level with the ground, and the natives were working for many days before they could clear away the débris from these wrecked homes."

Such are the storms which in our lonely Pioneer Mission Station we are doomed to experience during the month of April of each year, and it is indeed an exceedingly anxious time for all concerned whilst they last.

No sooner than the month of April is passed, the month of May brings with it an exceedingly hot sun, and is known amongst the natives as the month of the "Great Sun," there being very little rain and no storms worth mentioning. The heat is almost unbearable, but no sooner has June arrived than almost like clockwork the rains start to descend in earnest. The April storms have helped to usher in the Monsoon. During May the heavy clouds have been gathering all over the country, and whereas during the cold season the sky has been practically cloudless, the moon and the stars shining in all their glory, they are now hidden for the greater part of the rainy season behind the dense black clouds that continually roll over the sky.

The rainy season continues from the 1st of June until the 1st of October, and in Sherkor June and August being on the average the wettest months. During the rainy season one may expect from half an inch to seven inches of rain within the twenty-four hours, and on one special occasion it was our lot to experience a downfall of seven inches in the space of half an hour. Such an experience as this is exceedingly rare, and only happened to us on one occasion.

Having supplied ourselves with a rain gauge, we are enabled to take the fall of rain every twenty-four hours throughout the year and to keep a record of the same. Such a record may be of interest to our readers, and it is our great pleasure to publish the Lakher Rainfall for the first time in history.

RAINFALL AT SHERKOR, LAKHERLAND, FURTHER INDIA.

Name of Month.	YEAR.				Average of Three Years' fall of Rain for each respective month.
	1909.	1910.	1911.	1912.	
January . .	—	1·10	·47	·00	·52
February . .	—	·17	·00	·39	·19
March . . .	—	·01	2·63	4·60	2·41
April . . .	—	3·97	7·82	14·52	8·77
May . . .	—	5·97	11·52	9·81	9·10
June . . .	—	12·84	19·62	23·03	18·50
July . . .	12·43	13·33	15·27	—	13·68
August . .	22·99	13·56	15·34	—	17·30
September .	14·91	13·22	12·23	—	13·45
October . .	7·96	13·77	9·12	—	10·28
November. .	2·76	·66	·10	—	1·17
December . .	1·07	·00	·10	—	·39

Greatest Monthly Rainfall during the above three years, 23 inches (23·03).

Greatest Daily Rainfall (24 hours) during the above three years, 4¾ inches (4·65).

Yearly average of Rainfall for above three years, $95\frac{3}{4}$ inches (95·76).

The above figures are from observations taken at 8 a.m. each morning at the Lakher Pioneer Mission Station, Sherkor, Lakherland.

Throughout the rainy season tigers, which during the cold season are generally only found far away from human habitations, will at this season make their way to the environments of the villages, and are indeed a great source of trouble.

Every year round our lonely Mission station in Sherkor tigers frequently prowl within a stone's throw of the bungalow, carrying off any domestic animals that may cross their path, and during the space of six weeks we have known of a tiger carrying off no less than eight head of domestic animals, which were as follows :—

Three gayal,
Three full-grown pigs,
One goat,
One horse.

All these were seized at a distance of between two to five minutes' walk of our Mission bungalow. During this time one tiger was shot, but losses still went on, showing distinctly that this was the work of more than one beast.

Towards the end of this rainy season, the clouds having cleared from the sky, the moon was able to shed her soft rays over the jungle. At an hour near midnight the domestic gayal from the village came stampeding up towards our bungalow and forced their way into the front garden, their heavy bodies doing great damage.

Calling one of my native boys we set out together

to drive these huge creatures down the hillside towards the village which, with some difficulty, we soon accomplished, but on arriving at the foot of the hill down below us was a large female gayal who refused to budge, although large stones were continually pelted at her by ourselves, and for some ten minutes or more we endeavoured to drive this gayal, who appeared only as a shadow to us in the undergrowth of the jungle from her position, and at last we accomplished the feat and returned to our beds once again to sleep the rest of the night in peace.

In the morning, however, what was our surprise to find that the stubborn gayal who had refused to move for so long the night before had been standing over the dead carcase of her calf which had been struck down by a tiger and which she was evidently defending with great bravery, and the native and myself must have spent our time in not only pelting the gayal but in pelting the tiger himself, and it was quite evident that the cow gayal had not left her young one until the tiger had been forced to retreat, as the calf had only been bitten and killed by its enemy who had not dared to return to enjoy its meal.

On another occasion an old female tiger tore away the wall of our goat-house, which was situated at a distance of only about twenty yards from our bungalow. Tearing a hole in the bamboo-matted wall she forced her way through, and in entering smote a kid with her paw, then seizing one of our large milk goats she bounded out of the house once again, carrying her prey with her into the thick of the jungle. We found the kid in the morning smashed as flat as a pancake on the floor of the goat-house, showing the terrible power that these creatures have in their limbs.

My native helper "Saro" and myself built a platform about fifteen feet above the ground in the branches of a tree near by, and there we spent the whole of the following night waiting for the return of this monster, in the sincere hope of being able to bag her.

The night was very dark, but by the soft rays of the moon that every now and again broke through the heavy clouds we were able to distinguish for some little distance every object, and although we heard her prowling around, we were unfortunately unable to see her or to get in a shot, and were prone to come down from our platform in the early morning disappointed.

Two days after this, however, this same tiger killed two cows about a mile's distance in the jungle, and the owner of them with a friend sat up in a tree close at hand over the dead carcases awaiting the tiger's return to finish its meal. They had not long to wait. She came stealthily forward, and suspecting no danger started on her repast, when the sound of the firing of a bullet echoed and re-echoed through the jungle, and without a cry the monster rolled over stone dead.

She stood 3 feet at the withers and the footprints of her front paws were both 1 foot 6 inches in circumference, the two together forming the exact height which she stood at the withers herself. The measurement of the circumference of her skull under the throat and over the ears was also exactly 3 feet, and her length from her nose to the tip of her tail amounted to 8 feet 8 inches. She was an exceedingly old female, and one of her front paws bore the wound where a bullet had passed clean through at some former time, but had not caused her death. One of her fangs also was snapped off at the root, and there is no doubt that she found it an extremely hard matter to obtain her daily food amongst the wild animals of the jungle, and therefore had been daring enough to break through our goat-house so near to habitation as it was.

Such a thing as a man-eating tiger in Lakherland appears to be unknown, but some Lakhers have been mauled and killed by tigers when out in the depth of the jungle, but there is no knowledge of such a thing happening within the precincts of a village.

The rainy season is the great time of the year with the Lakhers for trapping wild animals, the ground being so sodden with the continual rains as to leave deep foot-prints behind any animal that has passed along, thus enabling them to know the best spots to place their various forms of traps. By far the commonest snared animal is the barking deer, and in order to catch these swift-paced animals, which are a little larger than a large-sized goat, they set a noose across the path, one end of which is tied to a bent-over bamboo or sapling, whilst the noose itself is hidden from view by the undergrowth. A fine line crossing the path is attached to a little trigger arrangement, and the unsuspecting deer comes bounding along and is bound to touch this fine line with its hoof, the slightest touch of which will release the trigger; the bent-over sapling being immediately freed from its lashings will spring into an erect position, drawing the noose tight about the unfortunate animal's head and the animal is suspended in mid-air strangled, until the setter of the noose comes along, and if not already dead, dispatches it.

Many animals, however, are killed by a trap on the principle of the bow and arrow, the arrow being a large bamboo sharpened to an exceedingly fine point, the other end of the shaft being tied to a long bamboo about 12 feet in length. This long bamboo acts as a spring; one end of it is placed between two posts which have been hammered securely into the ground, the other end having the arrow attached to it. A little platform of bamboos, which cannot be detected by the eye of the animal, is then made as a rest and guide for the arrow, and when this is complete a fine cord is placed across the pathway, at the end of which is a small trigger, also made of bamboo. The long bamboo containing the arrow is seized at the arrow end and bent back to the extent of some two feet, the trigger and cord being placed in a certain way so as to hold it in this position. According to the animal to be captured, so is the arrow placed at a height that is considered sufficient to strike its unfortunate victim in the heart.

The unsuspecting animal comes prowling along the road, and the slightest touch of its paw will release the trigger, and the already straining bamboo with its bamboo arrow attached will be released, and with an enormous force will strike the unfortunate beast, piercing its hide and going several inches into its body. Naturally the victim gives a bound and the arrow being secured by a cord to the long bamboo will not detach itself, and the animal is freed from the arrow. The wound, however, which is made, bleeding profusely, leaves a trail behind it, and if the setter of the trap has placed the position of the arrow correctly he will not have very far to follow this blood track before he finds his victim dead. If the arrow had not been attached to this bamboo, so the Lakhers say, but been allowed to pierce its victim, and the victim to escape with the arrow sticking into it, in all probability the wound would have healed up and the trapper would have lost his prize. The principle of this trap is very similar to the principle of the schoolboy shooting pellets of paper across the school-room from the end of his ruler while holding the other end firmly in his hand, and it goes by the name of "*Kâpu.*" This same trap is made in various sizes, according to the animal desired to be captured, being used more frequently in the obtaining of porcupines.

Traps for elephants are made by the digging of a large pit of sufficient size to admit one of these huge creatures. At the bottom of this pit a great number of sharp-pointed bamboos are stuck firmly in an upright position in the ground. The top is roofed in by boughs of trees and leaves and the animals are then driven towards these traps, and on their treading upon the weak roofing it gives way and the poor animal falls headlong into the pit, the short bamboos ofttimes causing the animal great torture. Once in the trap, however, it is soon dispatched, and the bones which contain the tusks are then carried to the village to decorate the front verandah. Where the British Government, however, has power, elephant hunting is now forbidden.

The Lakhers have a great number of smaller snares used for catching jungle fowl, peacock pheasants, black pheasants and the like which are numerous, but the general principle of them all is the bent-over sapling or bamboo, to form the power to draw the noose tight around the creature's neck.

There, however, is one other kind of trap which is often used and is formed by the falling of a log of wood on the victim's back, smashing it and wedging the victim under its heavy weight. This form is used for killing tigers, birds and even for rats, but it greatly damages game, smashing almost every bone in their bodies to splinters and bruising the flesh greatly.

Bird-lime for snaring small birds is also used, and is obtained from the juice of a species of rubber tree which is found throughout the country, and which when smeared on the branches of trees will secure any small bird easily, being soon dispatched by the trapper.

One other trap is worthy of mention and is used in catching jungle rats, porcupines and any boring animals. A long basket of bamboo lattice-work is made which is just sufficiently wide enough in diameter to admit of the animal passing along it. At one end it is closed, at the other end open. The open end is placed into the hole of the animal and supported by sticks of wood underneath and securely fastened. The porcupine or rat, as the case may be, on coming to the exit of its hole will observe the lattice basket, and finding no other way out will immediately commence to force its way through, believing that at the other end there is an exit. Once inside the basket it is impossible for the animal to turn. On it endeavouring to turn round, the lattice-work is plaited in such a way that it contracts and holds the body of the animal firm, making it only possible for the animal to go on, which, owing to the end being closed up, it is unable to do, and has no alternative but to wait there until its trapper dispatches it.

Jungle rats are very much appreciated by the people, who eat their flesh. Not troubling to skin the animals, they stick a skewer through their bodies, hold them over the flames of a fire which burns off all the hair and chars the skin, and is a sufficient cleansing for these people, who not only eat their flesh but eat their bones and their entrails as well, as a rule.

The difference between a jungle rat and a house rat is this. The house rat is brown all over, while the jungle rat has a snow-white belly.

There are several other species of rats in the country which are not as a rule eaten. Two are specially worthy of notice—the black rat which will kill your large fowls in a very short space of time and carry away your chicken in great numbers. The second species is the bamboo rat, which lives entirely on the roots of bamboos and is a much larger animal, generally the size of a young rabbit, with long incisor teeth with which it can cut through the toughest of bamboo roots. These rats are generally coloured, but one specimen which it was our privilege to obtain was snowy-white, the only specimen of its sort which we have ever seen.

Besides the Lakhers being keen huntsmen, they are also exceedingly fond of fishing, which for the greater part is carried out by means of traps. Most of these traps are very effective and catch large quantities of fish, and one special trap is of immense size and boasts of the name of "Chha." A strong dam made with felled trees is first of all placed across the river. Behind this are built large bins of plaited bamboo, each bin being filled with huge stones, and these act as supports to the dam and the bamboo lattice-work which is placed all the way along, reaching from the bottom of the river to several feet above the surface, the dam of logs themselves only reaching to within about a foot of the surface of the water. In this lattice-work are three large holes cut on a level with the water, and behind these large bamboo lattice baskets are placed, one exceedingly large one in the centre sometimes from 12 to 20 feet in length and several feet in diameter. The mouth of the basket is securely placed against the aperture in the lattice-work of the dam and firmly secured from being washed away. On either side of this basket are two other apertures, behind which two smaller baskets are placed and secured in the same manner.

This trap is only made at the termination of the rainy season when the waters in the rivers start to subside; the fish which yearly make their way up to the source of these rivers and there fatten and grow, at this time of the year start to make their way down towards the lower reaches. The dam of logs causing the water to slightly fall, and the volume of water just covering the apertures, the fish, finding the lattice-work obstruction in their way, swim along until they reach the apertures, where they are immediately swept through by the force of the water into the large bamboo baskets which are waiting to receive them, and there securely trapped, being unable to swim out again owing to the slight fall in the water which very effectively keeps the entrance closed.

Every forty-eight hours a band of Lakhers leave their village at this season and visit these traps, taking out the fish and placing them in their baskets to be carried up to the village to be consumed for food, carefully replacing the basket traps for the next haul.

Should, however, heavy rains occur, the river will again swell to an enormous extent, and the great amount of débris that is swept down on the exceedingly swift current will ofttimes sweep the whole trap away, and they are doomed to repeat the operation of building again. Such a disappointment generally occurs two or three times during September and October, the months in which these traps are of any use.

Very large fish at times are caught in this manner, weighing ten or twelve pounds apiece, and on one occasion we saw a large cat fish exceeding the size of a man and which required two men to carry it suspended on a pole, caught in one of these "Chha" traps.

Numerous other smaller traps are made very much on the same principle, and one trap which is used for catching crabs is very similar to those used among our fishermen in the homeland.

Besides trapping fish, a great deal is done by means of the hook and line, and many lines are set across the river having a number of hooks attached to them and baited with some dainty morsel, and Lakhers are not behind other native tribes in their appreciation of fish-hooks.

The use of the circular fishing net is also very common, and this is formed by a large circle of finely-knitted threads which, when spread out on the ground, would have a diameter of about 14 feet. In the centre of this circle a rope is securely tied, about 12 feet in length, and all round the circumference at very short intervals heavy leaden weights are fastened.

One end of the rope is seized in the one hand, while the other hand catches the knot in the centre where the other end of the rope is fastened. Lifting the net up in this manner the heavy weights immediately fall together, and then entering into the water for some little distance, in a very clever manner the Lakhers throw this net into the air, the weights immediately spreading the net out in a large circle and it falls on the surface of the water like a parachute, the water itself bearing up the finely-meshed cotton threads and the weights immediately sinking with great rapidity fall together under the water, and the net is immediately drawn to land by means of the rope, when every unfortunate fish that happened to be under the net at the moment of its striking the water is found securely caught, and with great rejoicing is placed in the native basket to be carried to the village in due course.

On one of our many excursions I decided to try my hand at fishing with this circular net, and after picking my way over great boulders on the river's brink, under the burning tropical sun, reached a convenient spot for the operation, and with high hopes of making a good haul I took the net in my hand in the manner I had seen my people do on many occasions and threw it into the air. It immediately opened with perfect accuracy, but before I had time to think I found myself headlong in the river, almost losing the net at the same time.

Struggling out, saturated to the skin, with my solatope as heavy as lead and my boots full of water, I decided that that should be my last effort at fishing with a circular net, and I would in future content myself with the humble civilized method of rod and line. As a reward for my energy I was obliged to take my boots from off my feet and place them on a stone to dry in the sun, beside my socks and shirt, keeping only my trousers and my sola-tope on me for the time being and having to undergo excruciating discomfort of walking over large stones heated in a sun of 96° in the shade and getting my body so sunburnt that for many days after I was not allowed to forget the little adventure.

By means of this circular net the Lakhers obtain the greater part of their fish food during the months intervening November and August when the river is either too low or too flooded to allow of trap-fishing with any great success.

Another mode of catching large quantities of fish is known as " Pa-ra-na Sa," which can be carried out only at certain periods in the rivers where an island divides the course of the river into two streams. At the lower end of the island on the narrowest stream a very strong lattice-work sieve-like bamboo, dam is fixed which allows all the water to pass through it. At the upper end of the island across the same stream a dam is built by felling a number of large trees, débris and stones helping to make it more effective, thus damming the entire flow of water and diverting it into the larger channel, the water in the smaller channel naturally flowing on through these sieve-like openings in the bamboo lattice-work and leaving the bed of the channel practically dry. The lattice-work has acted as a sieve through which none of the fish of any size were able to pass, and all that happened to be in this long channel are to be seen floundering about on the dry bed of the river and are swiftly gathered up, the dam at the upper end then being broken away sufficiently to allow the water to run in once again, and it is thus left for many days, after which the operation is repeated with like result.

Should the haul from any of these traps be a large one, the Lakhers immediately gather wood and light a number of camp fires along the river bank, sticking a split bamboo through the gills of their catch, string them up over the smoke of the fire, and in this way preserve them sufficiently to keep for several days until they arrive at their village, when they are placed over the fires in their huts, where they will keep for many months, being covered with soot and smoke the whole of the time.

The Lakhers are not water-men, and they own no boats of any kind, but should their fishing necessitate some means of getting out in mid-stream or crossing some large and unfordable river, they immediately resort to the bamboo, and felling a great number, which, after depositing them in the water, they tie together at one end very securely with cane ties, spreading out the other end in the form of a half-open fan, securing them in this position by means of cane ties and cross bamboos, and thus they have at hand a very practical raft, and one containing about a hundred bamboos of 15 feet in length is sufficiently buoyant to support two human beings, long bamboos being used as poles to propel the raft along. Should bamboos not be on the spot, wild plantain stems are sometimes used, three large stems being sufficient to hold one human being, but the bamboo raft is far preferable and has greater endurance, especially in any part of the river where treacherous rocks either under or above the surface are numerous.

The Lakhers as a nation are exceedingly fearful of travelling by water, and it takes a deal of persuasion to get a few men to go on an exploring expedition were rivers have to be navigated.

Where native paths are crossed by large rivers, it would generally be found, at any rate during the dry season, that the path has led to a ford in the river, but during the rainy season when the rivers are greatly swollen it would be impossible for any one to attempt to ford such a swift flow of water without surely meeting their doom.

At such places where owing to the width of the river it is impossible to build a native bridge, the Lakhers have a mode of ferry which is very ingenious, and on which principle numbers of ferries in the Homeland and in America are worked.

A bamboo raft as above described is made, to the front end of which a rope is attached about five feet long and having a large loop through which another large rope passes, the end of this rope being securely fastened on either side of the river round the trunk of some convenient tree. The passenger jumps on to the raft and catching hold of the taut rope securely in his hands causes the raft to stand at an acute angle with this rope. The force of the stream thus catching the raft on one side will force it across the river, carrying its burden with it. According to the angle in which the raft is pulled so is the direction in which the raft is driven, the head of the raft always standing towards the point started for.

Another long rope is also securely fastened to this raft which will reach to either shore, so that when the raft is abandoned by one traveller, it may easily be pulled across by any other traveller that may need it by means of this long rope. These ferries, however, are not often met with.

Far more numerous are the native bamboo bridges which were mentioned in the earlier part of this book, but there is another bridge worthy of mention which is made completely of cane instead of bamboo, and which can be made to stretch across a river where the erection of a bamboo bridge would be impossible. In all cases, however, these bridges are only sufficient for one to cross at a time, and the crossing is very much like walking a tight rope, the only redeeming feature about them being that rests are placed at the side which one may grip hold of to enable one to keep their balance, which is not an easy thing to any but a native with bare feet.

When out on hunting or fishing expeditions the Lakhers will ofttimes sleep in the open air of a night, selecting some smooth stone to act as a pillow, while when at home his pillow consists of a rounded piece of wood or a portion of a split giant bamboo which fits very conveniently into the nape of the neck, for the Lakhers never place their head proper upon a pillow, but place the pillow, which is always of the hardest material, under the nape of the neck.

When the rains, however, threaten a framework of bamboos, one end resting on the ground, the other end being raised by bamboo supports three or four feet, the whole then being covered over with large plantain leaves, will form an exceedingly comfortable camp for a night, and when lying down to sleep the Lakher will pull his large sheet securely over his head so that nothing is visible but, as it were, a bundle of clothes.

In this way he is enabled to sleep in comparative peace from the continual pestering of the numerous stinging insects which abound in large numbers and are exceedingly energetic, much to the discomfort of the weary traveller.

CHAPTER XIV

A CONSORT TRUE

LET us turn our attention once again to the actual Mission work amongst these interesting people.

The first two and a half years was exceedingly rough, uphill work. Situated in our little mountain home we were prone to many discomforts, and ofttimes not being able to obtain a Lakher native to work for us under any persuasion it fell to my lot to go down to the little stream and carry the heavy buckets of water from there—a quarter of a mile up the steep mountain side leading to our bungalow—many times during each day, for the spring was 400 feet below our home, and made the journey not only wearying but caused one to be thoroughly exhausted, not having been used to such rugged country.

Wood had to be fetched for the fire to cook by, and my brave little wife used to penetrate the jungle with me, gather and chop the dry sticks, placing them in bundles, whilst I carried them up the steep hillside; and there in the little bamboo cook-house with an open fire, the whole place being full of dense smoke, causing the eyes to smart and continually run with tears, stood my little wife day by day, cooking the meals and the bread, ofttimes having to rush out of the cook-house with eyes streaming with tears and intense pain through the smoke. How the natives can stand this constant volume of smoke is marvellous, but it very rarely seems to affect them in the slightest.

One of the hardest trials of my noble little housewife was the making of bread. Everything went well while the yeast behaved itself, which she made from bananas, but as soon as the rainy season commenced the yeast would continually go wrong and the bread refuse to rise, and even when the bread rose well, the cooking of it in a little native oven over an open grate was exceedingly exhausting, and it was not until some time after that we procured a packet of hops and made hop yeast that things went easier, for the hop yeast has always kept in perfect condition and yielded a satisfactory loaf. The next difficulty to be met was the washing question, for in India no white woman ever undertakes the washing, but all soiled linen is treated by the *Dhobi*. Here, however, far removed from civilization, no *Dhobi* was procurable, and it fell to the lot of my brave wife to undertake all this arduous work herself under the burning tropical sun, a matter which we have never been able up to the present time to obviate.

Without any help of any kind a great deal of our time was taken up in obtaining food and attending to the necessities of life. Furniture had to be made, our bamboo bungalow made home-like, and then as the cold season came on once again, we found the little children, who feel the change in the weather terribly, ofttimes hugging their shoulders, with their little naked bodies, pleading for something warm to put on, for the Lakher children, both boys and girls, up to the age of eleven and twelve, run about in a nude condition, with only a small cord tied round their wasts and a chain of beads round their necks, while their hair hangs down their backs in an unkempt condition.

Every moment of spare time, therefore, which the busy housewife could find was occupied with her sewing machine making little jackets for these dear little children that they might be kept warm. Every old dress or other piece of odd cloth that could be found was turned into a useful little garment, and these, needless to say, were exceedingly appreciated by them all.

When the men and women of the village and villages saw the usefulness of these little garments and what comfort they led to, great numbers of them used to ask to have one made for themselves, and it was soon obvious that the only way to at all cope with the necessities of the people was to charge some trifling sum for these garments, and so my wife made great numbers of them for the natives, supplying the cloth and all the work at the small cost of fourpence each. Where, however, the people could not find the fourpence to pay for them, work was offered, and as months passed by we managed to get some of them in this way to condescend to work, fetching bamboos or any other work that was necessary for the maintenance of the station.

Seeing the great advantage of the stitches of the sewing machine over the stitches which they made in sewing their strips of cloth together to form their large blankets, great numbers of the people would bring their own cloths from time to time that they might have them sewed in a neat manner. At first these were done free of charge, but the demands were so great that my busy wife was absolutely unable to cope with them, and we hit upon a plan of charging three eggs for every blanket sewn, which probably took half an hour in completing. In this way we were able to curtail their demands greatly, but ofttimes the whole afternoon and evening, and even up till near the midnight hour have I seen my wife turning away at her sewing machine in order to get some little jacket completed that this poor little boy or that dear little girl might not go another day shivering; and needless to say all these kind, tender sympathies of a white woman for her dark-skinned brothers and sisters were not wasted, but went an enormous way in helping the people to realize that we were their friends and not their enemies, and that there was glory in work and not glory in idleness as the Lakhers believed.

Day by day, note-book and pencil in hand, I would roam the village, visit the sick, and endeavour to catch every word that was uttered, placing them down again and again, with their probable English equivalents, asking the question times without number, "What is this?" or "What is that?" in order to obtain the name.

In this way, day by day, knowledge of the language was increased, but try as I would there was no opportunity of getting a native to help me with his language in any way. I, however, felt drawn towards a man whose name was "Saro," who lived at a village three days' journey from Sherkor, who from time to time would be at our village. Whenever I had the opportunity to be in his company I took every care to do so, for I saw in him a most intelligent being and the one whom I felt led to believe to be the very man I wanted.

Month by month slipped by, and I tried many

MRS. REGINALD A. LORRAIN (p. 199).

[To face p. 202.

times to persuade him to come and work at the language with me. He, however, had a wife who was very upset at his having anything to do with a white man, and whenever I prevailed upon him in the slightest manner to help me—for several times he was almost persuaded—she would immediately refute any such idea and he was lost to me again for some time.

After being in the country thirteen months, and being able to communicate slightly with the people in their own tongue, but fearing my knowledge of the language was so small I had never dared to preach the Unsearchable Riches of Christ to them, for the wrong pitch of the voice in the pronunciation of a word would entirely alter the meaning of words in many cases and would very probably give them other impressions than those I wished to convey.

I was strolling through the village one Saturday night when I was accosted by a loud feminine voice from the Chief's verandah, which lay at some little distance from where I stood. Going over to the place from whence the sound of the voice proceeded, I found the Chieftainess of "Siaha" village, two days' journey distance, squatting on the verandah, and on asking her why she had called me she said, "Will you come and tell us something about God's Word?"

I assured her that my knowledge of the language at that time was very inadequate to the occasion, but she insisted upon my doing so, and feeling there was nothing I could do but to do my best, I made up my mind, by God's Grace, to put into the best language at my command, something of the Love of our Heavenly Father, for Whose Glory we were in Sherkor.

Climbing up the log staircase I entered the verandah, and the hour-glass log stool was brought out for me to sit on, and in a very short time there must have been gathered together a crowd of some two hundred Lakhers, men and women, all ready to listen to what I might have to say. Praying to God for guidance, for help, and for strength at this critical moment, I started by singing a hymn, the only hymn which I had then composed in their language, and which later on I found necessary to revise owing to many errors in the translation. However, they listened very attentively, and after the singing of this hymn I stood there in the midst of this large gathering of natives, not in my own strength but in His, and as I started to tell them of the great Love that God had for mankind and for the Lakhers, about how His Son Jesus Christ had left all in Glory to come and tell us of the Fatherhood of God, and how He had died upon Calvary that they might live and that spiritual light might come into their souls, I found to my utter surprise that my lips, as it were, were loosed and I was enabled in that hour to speak in their native tongue in such a way that I never had had the power to do before.

God certainly had blessed the endeavour, and He had helped, He had opened my mouth and had given me the gift of tongues, not in the faint babbling of unmeaning barbaric words before an audience amongst whom not one could understand, but through the constant endeavour to obtain the knowledge of the language in an exceedingly short time without the aid of books, without the aid of a human helper, but by the aid of the Holy Spirit Himself, Who has promised to be our teacher not only in the ways of life, but in all our undertakings. He had blessed the endeavour and given the Power at this time of need, and by their faces and by their attention one could see that a greater part at any rate was entering into their minds and that they understood to some great extent what was said.

This was a Red Letter Day for Lakherland. The first day throughout all human history that the Love of God had ever been spoken in the Lakher tongue.

From that day forth we started our meetings amongst these people, and on the following day we had another glorious meeting with a large audience, and several times each week my dear wife and myself used to wend our way through the village, and "Thylai," the Chief, having given us permission to use his verandah for our meetings, we continued to tell these people something of that love which had bought them and was seeking them, and was waiting to receive them, into the Fold.

Some little time after the commencement of these meetings, we had for various reasons been unable to get down to the village so often, and on passing through one morning we came to the Chief's house and enquired how he was, and were surprised to find that he was ill. Entering into the large hut, we found him lying on a bamboo bed raised about four inches from the floor, by the side of a log fire, exceedingly exhausted, and we learned that for ten days he had been getting weaker and weaker. There were beer pots close by and numbers of Lakher men sucking their beer through the bamboo straws, talking one against the other and making an enormous noise.

On examination we found that he was in a very bad condition and exceedingly weak, but we asked him if he would take our medicine instead of sacrificing to the evil spirits, and allow us to pray with him, which he willingly did. After giving him his medicine, my wife and self knelt down beside the prostrate body and asked God, for Christ's Sake, to bless the drug, and if it was His will, to spare his life, and to teach him the way of Salvation.

Day by day we tended that Chief in his dingy, sooty hut, and as the Lakhers consider the drinking of milk as a pernicious habit, they will on no consideration drink it if they know it to be such, but we could see that there was no doubt that this poor Chief was starving to death through want of proper food as well as suffering from other ills. Day by day my wife would give him milk to drink, but he had to take it under the name of medicine without any knowledge that it ever belonged to the cow, and ofttimes we found it was necessary to place a small crystal of permanganate into it to give it a slightly different colour so that it should not be recognized as milk; each time medicine was administered a blessing was asked of God.

One day, on entering the hut, I found it crowded inside with a great number of men drinking at a large number of beer pots, talking one against the other and making an awful bedlam, discussing one with the other what they should do with his body when he died, who should be their Chief, and many other very obnoxious questions for the dying man.

I expostulated with them and tried to point out how wrong it was of them to do such things, but they told me in his hearing that he was an old man and they wanted him to die that his young son might reign in his stead, and raised objections to our giving him medicine and nursing him day by day. However, it was the Lord's will that he should not die, and in the course of a short time he became quite well and was able to go about his village again, much to his great joy, but there were a number of men in that village who were not a little displeased at our having been the means of saving their old Chief, which they showed in many ways. The Chief, however, was very thankful, and from that time forth he was exceedingly friendly with ourselves and the work, and in any way possible he would help us by lending us his verandah or the flat piece of ground in front of his dwelling to hold our services, whilst on the other hand his wife has always showed herself very adverse to Christianity, and on one occasion I heard the old Chief say, "I would like to become a Christian myself, but my wife won't have anything to do with it."

After having been eighteen months in the country, I decided that I would make a special effort to persuade "Saro" to become my helper, in order that the now large number of words which I had managed to gather together might be verified, and the dictionary, which it was my intention to compile, started.

Saddling our ponies we made a tour to his village, three days' journey away, visiting the villages by the wayside and holding several meetings in each of them, having large audiences of men, women and children gathered round us at all these meetings, where we taught them the words of the two hymns which we had now been able to place in their language, the second one being,

> What can wash away my stain?
> Nothing but the Blood of Jesus.

At these meetings many of those gathered round

afterwards entered into conversation, asking many questions about God and His Love, the future estate of all those that love and follow Him, and we had a very beneficial and interesting journey, but the day's marches were exceedingly tedious, the roads over the hills being little more than tracks, and our ponies ofttimes finding it exceedingly hard to pick their way up the inclines, whilst we ourselves in many cases had to help them by going ahead and keeping firmly hold of the reins.

At last we arrived at "Tisôpi" village where "Saro" and his family lived.

The Chief came out to meet us and invited us to hold a meeting on his verandah, and although exceedingly tired and worn out with the day's march, we felt it our duty to do so, as we intended to go on very early the next morning to a village still one day's journey further afield. At this meeting we had a very enthusiastic gathering, men, women and children being gathered on the verandah and on the little piece of level ground outside the hut, listening intently to every word which was spoken, Saro standing amongst them; and where several of the old people were not able to catch all the words which I spoke, I heard him telling them again so that they were distinctly able to understand.

After the meeting we retired to our night's abode, and much to our joy we found that Saro was quite willing to come in and help, and he gave me a definite promise to that effect, promising to arrive at the beginning of the following month.

His wife, who had always been very opposed to his coming, was no less opposed on this occasion, and refused to enter into conversation with me, but on the following morning we moved on to "Phiahra"

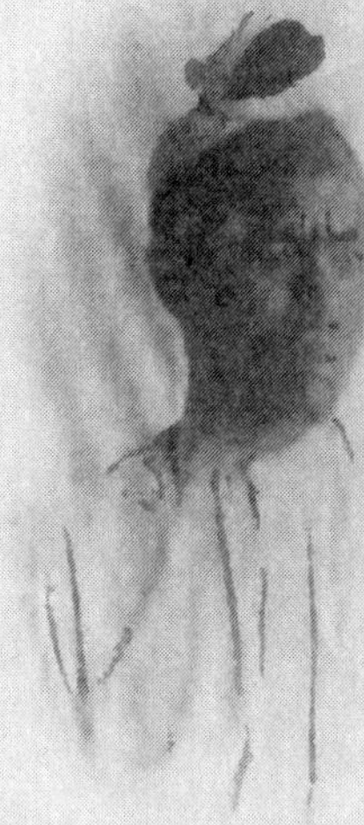

"Saro,"
the faithful native helper (p. 211).

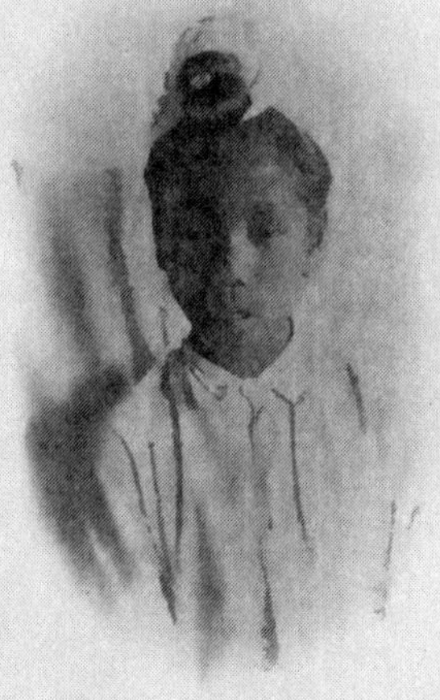

"Thytu,"
the first convert to Christianity (p. 236).

"Chiahu,"
the second convert to Christianity (p. 236).

TYPES OF LAKHER MEN.

[*To face p.* 208.

village, where we held large open-air meetings, and on the morning following we returned direct to Sherkor, holding meetings every afternoon and evening at the various villages, arriving home after an absence of eight days.

The time came at last for Saro to arrive, but instead of himself appearing he sent a message of excuse, but after some time, various messages passing between us, he decided he would keep his promise and ultimately came in to become my helper.

No sooner had he taken the definite step than his wife divorced him, but it was evident that he was not much attached to her, and it did not cause him much regret at her decision, for he soon after took another wife in Sherkor village, built himself a hut, and settled down there. Thus God provided me with a helper, a man who has proved invaluable to the advancement of the Kingdom of Christ in that land.

First of all I had to teach him how to read and write in the Lakher language, and he very soon mastered the art; and with his aid, day by day, sitting close at the study table for five or six hours, he has been faithful and learned to know exactly what I was driving at.

Day by day the vocabulary of the language increased, each word being written on a separate square of paper with the English equivalent, which had periodically to be strictly alphabetically arranged and to be alternately entered into the English and Lakher dictionary, a work which used to take the whole of every evening, sometimes surpassing the midnight hour. All the work that I had been enabled to accomplish during the day had to be entered up and finished before the night's rest could be claimed, and my patient and devoted wife would sit at the opposite side of the table under the light of the lamp, busily making little garments for the native children or at some other work of love. As the months passed by the work naturally increased, and after the starting up of a school of Lakher Tribesmen to teach them to read and write, the work became almost beyond our reach, and naturally in order to keep pace with this ever-increasing work the days had to be lengthened and the nights shortened. Besides the work at the dictionaries of the language grammatical notes had to be kept until at last in 1910 a complete grammar of the Lakher language was made which entailed a great deal of mental fatigue.

Naturally we were anxious to give to these people a portion at any rate of the Word of God, and as some of these Lakher tribesmen in our school became able to read and write in their own language, it was necessary that they should have something to read, and what could be better than a Gospel in their hands, which read and re-read would each time throw greater light into their lives, although the reading would ultimately become old to them, yet the Word would still remain Ever New.

Thus I determined after much prayer and consideration to commence on the translation of the "Gospel according to St. John," and to those who have never translated the Scriptures from one language into another, the enormous task and problems that it entails cannot be appreciated in the slightest degree. Some days I was able to translate quite a long paragraph, when some small word would stand in the way as a huge barrier, and it would take hours to overcome it. Thus day by day the work went on slowly but surely, by the guidance of God chapter by chapter was completed, and as each chapter came to completion it was handed over to the boys in the school and each one of them that could read and write had to copy it out in his own handwriting in an exercise book supplied for that purpose, a feat which they exceedingly well executed, and these chapters were read and re-read by these boys and men over and over again until a new chapter should be completed. Thus the greater part of the boys in the school have written out completely the whole of the "Gospel of St. John" in their own handwriting, and God has blessed the reading of His word to their souls as will be seen later.

The Gospel being at last completed, I felt it was better to have one Gospel as perfect as possible in its translation rather than to turn my thoughts to others, and ere I was satisfied with the ultimate translation of the Gospel I found I had revised it no less than five times, carefully going over every word and every sentence with a number of books of reference on my table.

During all these tedious months Saro remained exceedingly faithful to the work, and not only faithful was he but he became interested, and deserves to be termed a co-worker with myself in giving to his nation the Wonderful Words of Life.

It must be remembered that these people are no lovers of indoor life, but are used to roaming the jungle and spending the greater part of their existence in the open air, and for a man of this description a d with all the instinct of a savage to remain contented, to sit close at a study table for many hours each day that the work might be completed, shows, I believe, that God was working in his heart and that Jesus Christ Himself was with us as we tackled those knotty problems in His name.

We had now reduced the Lakher language to writing for the first time in the history of the world, and were in the thick of compiling two bulky dictionaries in the language, whilst the grammar was just completed, and besides this St. John's Gospel was in hand. Still the needs of the Mission called for more, and our thoughts had to turn to the great needs of a hymn-book, a need which was pressing itself very much to the front, and much time had to be given to reducing a selection of well-known English hymns into words suitable to the language; and in the course of time we had a little hymnal ready for the press of some thirty-seven selections, which a few friends in the Homeland made it possible for us to place in print and which proved a mighty weapon, bringing home to the hearts of those within our reach the wonderful Love of God.

We still lacked, however, a primer for the school work, lessons having to be written and re-written out on separate sheets of paper and on the blackboard day by day which swallowed up an enormous amount of valuable time which we could ill afford to lose. Thus I set myself the task of compiling a suitable primer to reach the needs of these people in order that they might learn to read and write in their own language, which was duly completed, while the Government of Assam were kind enough to print it for the Mission free of charge; and this little book has been one of the greatest aids in initiating the Lakher tribesmen into the mysteries of reading and writing, thus forming the first step towards their learning to read the good news of the Gospel of Salvation.

With all these pressing duties, some time out of each day was taken up with the medical work, numbers of patients visiting our dispensary and asking relief for their various ills, and all who came were supplied from the dispensary, where possible, with a cure, while in other cases relief was afforded, for the Lakhers are a semi-syphilitic tribe and their sores ofttimes were exceedingly loathsome, and in such cases as these nothing but relief for the time being could be given.

From time to time it was our custom to go round the village and visit those who were sick, administering medicine and praying with them as necessity called, and in this way many sick persons were relieved of their pain, not through the power of the medicine only, but by the power of God working through the medicine to His own Glory and Honour and to the establishment of the confidence of the natives in us.

One case is specially worthy of note, and which shows distinctly what a powerful weapon the Missionary has in his hand in the form of scientific medical knowledge.

One evening, after an arduous day's toil, and having finished our cup of tea, my wife and myself decided to take a stroll through the village in the way of exercise, the first time for several days. At the beginning of the village was an extra large size hut belonging to one of the head-men of the village. It was getting dusk and a bright log fire which was burning on the flat ground outside the hut first attracted our attention, and on drawing near we found in the customary manner that the house was barricaded around by a tiny railing of bamboo, whilst on the fire stood a large iron bowl with something boiling in it, and by the side squatted a man busy at cutting up a freshly-killed pig, which piece by piece he threw into the boiling liquid.

Seeing at once that there was a special sacrifice being offered for some sick person, I enquired the reason for the sacrifice, asking who it was that was ill. Ofttimes at such sacrifices none of the people concerned will condescend to answer, as they are bound to perfect silence for a period of about twenty-four hours. This time, however, the owner of the house recognized my voice, and immediately stepped outside the hut and gave us an answer to my question, informing us that his little son, some few years of age, was lying at death's door and that for several days he had been offering sacrifices to the evil spirits in order that they might be appeased and that his son might live, but "To-night," he said, "I am sacrificing a full-grown pig, one of the last of my domestic animals that I have, in the sincere hope that the evil spirits will accept this great sacrifice and spare my child's life. I have nothing more to sacrifice, but up to the present time the evil spirits will not listen to my cry."

I asked him why he had not sent up for medicine instead of sacrificing so many of his domestic animals, and why he had not trusted in God rather than the Devil. He shrugged his shoulders and gave me no answer. I then told him that according to their laws and customs no one was allowed to step over that little bamboo barricade during a sacrifice, and that I had not come into their country to go against their laws, but on the other hand if he would undertake to clear away the whole paraphernalia and throw it down the precipice, on the crest of which his house was built, I would then enter his hut, give his little one medicine and pray to Jehovah that He, for the sake of Jesus Christ, would spare his little son's life.

The man paced his verandah to and fro for several minutes with his arms folded, in deep thought, and then to our utter surprise he turned round to the man who was busy dissecting the pig which had been sacrificed and told him to clear away the whole sacrificial furniture and throw it down the precipice in order that we might enter the dwelling and try to help his little boy.

This act was an exceedingly brave one, for it practically defied the evil spirits to the utmost and showed a spirit full of faith in the Power of the Almighty, Jehovah.

We entered his hut, and there sitting in the centre close to the fire was a woman, the mother of the infant, whilst in her arms stretched out stiff and to all appearances on the point of death was the little one himself, whilst around her also squatting on the bamboo floor were numbers of relatives and members of the family.

Carefully examining the little one we found it to be suffering from Pneumonia, and when we looked upon its little face and saw the condition it was in and thought of how many days it had been neglected and not given proper treatment, our faith for its recovery was exceedingly small, and from every human standpoint we believed that the little one must pass away that night.

Having in my pocket a small bottle of Brionia I gave him half a pilule, leaving three other half pilules each wrapped in separate papers with the mother, to be given at a period of every three hours during the night. After administering this half pilule my wife and myself knelt down beside that mother and her little infant and prayed that God might honour the faith of this man who had thrown away his sacrifice, thus defying the evil spirits and placing his trust in Jehovah, that He might honour that faith and show forth His Wondrous Power to save.

During this prayer not a murmur was made, but all listened very intently. Then we rose to our feet and bade them good-night, instructing them once again about giving the other doses at the proper times, and wended our way up the mountain side to our bungalow.

This was Saturday night, and on the Sunday morning we went down the very first thing to visit the little one and to see how he was getting on, and found him greatly improved, and during our Sunday service we made his life a special matter of prayer, and all those gathered at that service heard the request that the little one might be spared yet a little longer, and marvellous to relate in the course of about only four days that little one was apparently quite himself again, and the father naturally was not a little pleased and thankful.

The incident had passed away and several months had come between, when on one Sunday afternoon I decided to hold an open air meeting in the village in the midst of a huge beer-drinking bout that was then in progress.

On the level ground in front of the Chief's house were a great number of beer pots. Gathered around these were large circles of men, talking one against the other at the very top of their voices, each taking their turn at pulling at the sweet rice beer, each time becoming more heated in their arguments, whilst round the whole group were gathered numbers of children and women. Pigs in great number wended their way through these circles, the horrible yelping village curs continually fighting one another in the midst, and for their trouble had many a log of wood hurled at them full force from some man's hand, whilst the hens and the cocks were cackling and crowing to their hearts' content, and the noise was indeed deafening.

Such was the very unfavourable-looking position we had chosen for our Sunday afternoon meeting with the object of pointing these savage men to a life of joy in Christ Jesus.

Taking up our position in a convenient spot amongst them, we took one of our large Scripture pictures and hung it up on a stick so that all might see it and examine it to their hearts' content, and then with one or two bright hymns and a short prayer for God's blessing on what was about to be said, I rose from my little stool and started on the old theme of God's Love for them, that He had given His Son Jesus Christ to die in their stead, and pointed out to the best of my ability how that they were striving in the wrong way and in the wrong path, how to get the best out of life, leading them to the foot of the Cross and pleading with them to think of the Wonderful Words of Life which Jehovah in His wonderful love and kindness towards them had sent to them through ourselves, and pointing out very definitely to them the difference between ourselves and the Great Love of the Almighty God in sparing His Son Jesus Christ to die for them, who through sin were the enemies of God, and in the Great Love of Jesus Christ in offering up Himself as a willing sacrifice in their stead that they might live if they would only repent and turn to the Only True and Living God, Whom to know is Life Eternal.

During this little discourse the man whose son had been so marvellously saved from death, and who had thrown away his sacrifice in order that we might enter into his hut, jumped up and immediately drew the attention of all those Lakher men, women and children gathered at that large feast. Throwing his large blanket across his shoulder, he addressed them thus :—

"All you men of Sherkor have been listening to what 'Pâpu' (myself) has been saying. Now just you listen to me for a minute. There must be something very real and very true in these words of the love which God has for us, and how that Jehovah is the only true and living God, and of the love of Jesus Christ in sending forth to this far-off land these white people to tell us that Great Love. Now, as you all know, my son was dying some little time back, and after sacrificing to the evil spirits nearly all my domestic animals with no avail, while sacrificing a large pig Pâpu and Pâpi (my wife) told me that if I would cast the whole sacrifice away and trust in Jehovah, that He might, for Christ's sake, accept my faith and heal my boy.

"After considering for a little time I cast the whole of my sacrificial furniture down the precipice, and Pâpu and Pâpi entered into my hut where they saw my little one lying stiffened out almost dead in its mother's arms. They gave it some medicine and there in my house prayed to Jehovah, for Christ's sake, to spare my little son and to accept my faith in throwing away the sacrifice, thus defying the evil spirits, and on the following day at their meeting they prayed that my little boy might be spared, and in a very few days he was quite well.

"Had I kept to the sacrifice, and not thrown away my sacrificial furniture, I am certain that he could never have lived. Thus I say that it is evident there must be a great deal of truth in the Power of Jehovah and in the love of Jesus Christ for us."

With this he sat down, and during the whole of his discourse not a sound was to be heard. All was silence, and every one there present realized that this man was testifying to the truth.

A heathen man in the midst of the whirl of that drinking bout felt bound to make his voice heard and to tell out what had actually happened to his own family, the details of which all present were bound to acknowledge were correct. But it is not easy for these people to acknowledge the Lord Jesus Christ as their Saviour, for the pressure brought to bear upon them by their home circles and other relatives is very great, especially from their wives; and this man has never accepted the Lord Jesus Christ as his Saviour to the present time, but we trust and pray as the years pass by he too may be brought into the Kingdom, and that the Joy Bells of Heaven may be rung once again, that he to whom the Lord was so merciful at that time has at last not only acknowledged that mercy but has received the very Gift of His Salvation through Jesus Christ.

But a witness like this amongst a savage people will not easily be forgotten, and in the saving of that little boy's life it may be that God had a far greater object in view than the mere fact of acknowledging the man's faith; and it may be as years go by lives then influenced will be unwittingly drawn into the Gospel Net and be claimed from the very depths of heathenism, to sparkle in the Crown of the King of Kings, to stand round His Throne and tell the wonderful story Saved by Grace.

Our medical work has been a great lever in reaching these people, in gaining their confidence and in getting in touch with their families, and has given us the great privilege of being enabled to introduce into their homes the realization of the Power of Prayer, and although there have been many cases where our medical aid has been absolutely refused, in numbers of these cases death has ensued, but on the other hand a greater number of homes have pleaded for our help, and throughout the whole of our experience in that land, wherever a home has given up the sacrificing to evil spirits and have placed their trust in the Power of God through our medicine, the Mission has yet to record the first life to have been lost; and in this way the people have been reached, their homes visited, their thoughts turned towards the most marvellous thing in their minds that we should care for a dying man or endeavour to help another who may be in any need, for the Lakhers, as a rule, will seldom help a neighbour, certainly not if they can shift the responsibility upon some one else. In numbers of cases I have known of the nearest relatives and sometimes the children themselves refusing to walk half a mile in order to fetch medicine for an invalid mother or father, aunt or uncle, brother, sister or cousin, who themselves were absolutely unable to move, thus showing their absolute alienation from true love, for while a mother has a great affection for her infant, yet no sooner does that infant grow up to be a little child of seven or eight, than the only thought of the parents towards that child, as a rule, is how much work they can get out of it on their farms, and they practically lose control over their children after this age; should they die they experience a grief, but it is in no way as deep and as real as the grief which civilized people are called to experience.

This, however, becomes changed to some measure in those who have passed through our school, and in our converts, in whom a great change is being manifest, and in their daily life we have noticed in many ways they have endeavoured even to their own disadvantage to help some of their fellow-countrymen, thus showing that as soon as the Love of God enters into the soul that soul is regenerated. It becomes a new creature in Christ Jesus, for God is Love, the Source and Creator of Love, and without the knowledge of the Only True God there is no true experience of love and its power in and over the soul.

CHAPTER XV

TRAINING A SAVAGE

ON our arrival in Lakherland on September 26, 1907, a work lay before us which, humanly speaking, had insurmountable difficulties—no written language, no book to which to turn for reference, nothing but the rawest of material to work upon, without so much as a bungalow in which to live, save for the tiny hut which we occupied during the first months of our sojourn.

Nevertheless the Lord had called, God's Voice had spoken in accents so plain and He had opened up in such a marvellous way the door into the Lakher country, that we felt convinced that the great difficulties which stared us in the face day by day in His strength could be overcome, and that victory was sure to be ours, for the Power which was on our side was stronger than all that could be against us.

After having resided in the country for six months we endeavoured to find four little boys belonging to a neighbouring tribe of Lushais, and these we took under our care for the time being, teaching them to read and write in the Lushai language which we now had a fair knowledge of. Very shortly, however, these four boys were increased to eleven, seven of which were of the " Lushai " tribe and four others belonged to the " Chin " or " Poi " tribes.

After two months and a half, however, all these boys removed from Lakherland to their own country amongst their own peoples for various reasons, and we were left without any schoolboys, the Lakhers up to this time not caring to enter our school. We were not sorry, however, for this break up, as we had not come into the country to do work in the Lushai language, and our only object in starting this school had been to act as a lever in drawing some Lakher children under our care and supervision.

While these boys were in school, however, they very speedily advanced in knowledge, for on entering they could neither read or write for the greater part, but during their short stay at school they went completely through their Lushai primer, and on leaving could read and write sufficiently in the Lushai language to enable them to read their Gospel slowly. One or two of the boys, however, had already gained a slight knowledge of reading and writing from the B.M.S. Mission Station, seven days' journey north of us, but they greatly advanced in their powers during this short stay at the school.

Two days after the closing down of these classes, we were working in the cool of the evening, making our front garden look a little more homely and enticing, when we were accosted by two Lakher tribesmen, both being of about the age of twenty years, whose names were "Mawkha" and "Laihno," and who had come in two days' journey from their village "Siaha" and asked if we would teach them to read and write in their own language.

This was just what we had been praying for for some time past, and no doubt many of our friends in the Homeland had joined us in these prayers as well, and at the appointed time here we had two Lakhers expressing a desire to branch out into the knowledge of reading and writing.

We took them in and promised them their food as long as they stayed at school, as it was impossible for them to obtain such in Sherkor village. For one week these boys studied the Lakher alphabet, and there only being two of them they became exceedingly lonesome, we not having a room available in which to hold our school it had to be held on the verandah, and being the commencement of the rainy season it ofttimes proved exceedingly uncomfortable for all of us, so they asked that they might be allowed to go to their village for a little holiday, promising to return again shortly.

They did so, but in three weeks' time they were back again, not by themselves only, but accompanied by a friend who also wished to be included amongst the number; and so for another short period the school was continued once again and then another holiday was asked for which we granted, and our three boys, who by this time could spell out their words and pronounce them, returned to their village.

It was not long, however, before the Government Officials at Lungleh and Aijal, seven and fifteen days' journey from us respectively, realizing the good of such work, offered us some coolies if we would undertake the building of a new school-house, for which we were very thankful.

In due course the first school-house in Lakherland was completed, built on a convenient spot between our bungalow and the village. It was about 25 feet long and 15 feet across and had two little class-rooms on either side at the further end, which made the plan of the building like the letter "T";

The First School-house in Lakher-land (*p.* 224).

A village street showing stone graves and wooden monumental posts (*p.* 160).

[*To face p.* 224.

and then to give it a peculiarity of its own, and as we intended to use the school-house also as a church as well, we constructed a small spire of bamboo mat-work at the front end, whilst close at hand two native huts were built in which the schoolboys were to live while residing at school.

On August 24, 1908, we re-opened our school, not with three boys as before, but on their return they had brought with them others, and our number now swelled to six. By the middle of September our numbers had increased to eleven, and although the funds at our command were exceedingly small, yet my wife and myself agreed that as long as we could possibly manage to do so, not a Lakher tribesman should be refused the opportunity of learning to read and write in order that he might be able to read the Word of God.

A special appeal was made for this work in the Official Organ of the Mission, *Notes from Lakherland*, at this time, but it fell on practically deaf ears, and at the beginning of the following November we were obliged to close down our school for many months owing to the dearth of funds.

In our opinion it was a great pity and a great set back in the work, and at that time the outlook was exceedingly dark.

For ten and a half months the school had closed doors: the sound of a hymn from the schoolboys' voices could not be heard, the voices that mumbled the mysterious letters that form their alphabet were silent, daily united prayer on behalf of their fellow-tribesmen had ceased because there was no gathering together, and for one reason only, and that the non-realization of the responsibility that rests upon those in the Homeland in Holding the Ropes, in supplying the need, first by their sincere prayer and then by their pecuniary help.

That ten and a half months of seeming darkness, however, had one redeeming feature—it gave to me the whole of my time to devote all my energies to reducing the language to book-form, to study hard at the compiling of the dictionaries, and start the translation work of "The Gospel of St. John."

On September 13, 1909, that darkness was dispersed by a gleam of light, and four Lakher tribesmen, three of whom were old scholars, having expressed a great desire to return to school and there to learn more of God's Word, we decided to re-open once again. Four weeks after this these four boys were increased to seven. In another three weeks they had grown to ten. In another two weeks twelve were on our roll. In another week these twelve boys had swelled to sixteen, and as Christmas was drawing close at hand we decided to send them back to their villages for six weeks' holiday in order that we should be able more easily to meet their needs in the coming year.

In the following February we re-opened our school, thirteen boys returning. Before the end of the year our school had swelled to twenty-two boys, one boy by this time having completed his year's training at school. This boy was the son of an influential Chief residing at "Tisôpi" village, and who one day in all probability will become an influential Chief himself. This man, whose name is "Riatô," and who has now a wife and a little child, sent me a letter some little time back, beautifully written in his own language, into which he placed a very short sentence to this effect :—

"*I am continually thinking of what I was taught*

Two Lakher boys, "Lailia" and "Chiahu," as they were on entering the Mission School.

The same two boys after a short training at the Mission School.

SONS OF HEAD-HUNTERS (*p.* 230).

[*To face p.* 226.

in the school about Jehovah and Jesus Christ our Saviour, and I don't forget to pray daily, and it is by the Grace of God and your good will that I keep in perfect health."

These few words show the influence that has been brought to bear upon the heart and mind of this man during his year's stay in the Lakher school, where he had received not only the knowledge of reading and writing, but had learned to know a great deal of God's Word and had come under the power of Christian Influence for the whole of that twelve months, cut off from all his heathen rites and ceremonies, unable to offer sacrifices to the evil spirits, trusting on the Lord to keep him in health and strength while at school, constantly coming under the power of united prayer in our meetings this man had started to pray for himself.

Surely there is rejoicing in the Heavens for such a sign as this in the heart of a heathen man, and although this man has not up to the present asked to be placed on the Christian Roll, yet the Lord who reads the hearts knows all, and " God works in a mysterious way, His wonders to perform," and there is every hope that one day we shall have the pleasure of seeing the name of " Riatô " on the Christian register as an out and out follower of the Son of Man.

Christmas again coming round, we closed down for a short holiday, and in the coming year we hit upon an entirely new plan of school work, allowing four boys to go away for a holiday at a time, thus giving each boy about two months' holiday during the year, the school, however, never ceasing its work but continuing month by month. This enabled us to meet the needs of these boys, and to give them every opportunity of being grounded in reading, writing and simple arithmetic, nearly all the boys in the school also learning by heart the whole of the little volume of "Questions and Answers on the Story of God's Plan of Salvation from Genesis to Revelation," which we had been enabled to compile, each one writing it out, and not having been able to have it printed, each one had to write out his daily portion day by day until it was in their possession for future reading as well as being in their minds.

At the commencement of this year's schooling we started with sixteen boys, many having left school after the year's course, but this was soon increased to twenty-one boys.

A few of the friends in the Homeland had taken the cause of these Lakher tribesmen to heart and supported their own schoolboy at a cost of £3 a year, the Government of India also allowing the Mission a grant for four boys a year, but the balance of the school had to be met from our own slender purses and was ofttimes a great burden, but God in His great mercy enabled us in one way and another never to turn away any Lakher tribesman who expressed a desire to learn. Had, however, the funds at our command been greater, with a very little persuasion we could have managed to have increased our school to large numbers, and the work would have advanced with greater rapidity.

How often would we have liked to have transplanted some who bear the Name of Christ in the Homeland, as it were by magic, into the midst of these people hungering after Salvation and knowledge; and could such a thing have been done, how deep would the hands have been dipped in the pocket in order that these hungering souls might have had the opportunity given to them to feed on the Bread of Life. How oft would those round golden coins have jingled in the ear of their owner, asking how long were they to be imprisoned in their case of cloth and deprived from bringing some poor lost soul into the Glorious Light of the Gospel of Jesus Christ.

How greatly has God blessed many of his people with the enormous wealth of this world, but how often are these glittering coins unconsecrated to the work in the Master's vineyard. The sickle is there, but it lies rusty and corroded for the want of use.

> "Thrust in thy sickle and reap,
> For the hour to reap has come;
> The Harvest of the Lord is ripe,
> Thrust in thy golden sickle bright,
> And sing the Harvest Home."

How are these Lakher tribesmen cared for? How are they taught? What is the influence under which they come, and what will be the issue of all their training? are a few interesting thoughts which we might consider with advantage.

In the first place there is a comfortable school-house which consists of a building without any seats, and for the greater part the boys (for we call both men and boys, however old or however young they may be, schoolboys, and they range from the age of ten years to thirty-five years or more) squat on the ground, but there are ranged along the walls for those who care to use them small boxes which act as stools. These are small, easily stacked away, and convenient, whilst the walls of the schoolroom are decorated with coloured Scriptural pictures.

Besides this, at a little distance, there is a large house built on piles after native fashion for these boys to sleep in of a night, on entering which we shall see on the one side a long bamboo platform raised about two feet from the ground which acts as their bed, on which the boys, each with his own hard wood or bamboo pillow, lie, not with their heads to the wall as one would imagine, but with their feet to the wall and with their heads turned towards the centre of the hut. At one end is a large fireplace with a bright fire burning in the hearth, and the smoke curling along the roof finding its exit through any chinks in the bamboo walls.

Suspended from the roof of the hut is a long bamboo on which the boys hang their shirts and cloths to dry should they manage to get them wet, and above the bed at the head end is a long bamboo shelf divided off into sections, one section for each boy, where he keeps his various treasures, whilst all around pasted on the walls of the house may be seen various kinds of pictures which they collect from us from time to time.

Each boy has a certain duty to perform every day of the week in turn. One or two of them are allotted off for sweeping out the house daily, another band are allotted off to fetch the water for all the boys, another band to fetch the wood, and these bands change over from week to week, so that all take their full share of the work. One boy is placed as their head, and any failure in cleaning out the school-house or their own has to be reported by the Head Boy; should it not be reported and should come to my knowledge, then the head boy has to take the whole of the blame. Needless to say, these few rules and regulations are not arduous, and the boys have the greatest freedom that it is possible to allow them for the general good opinion of the school, and they live month in and month out in the greatest of friendship one with the other and are indeed very happy. The head boy, at five minutes to seven in the morning, comes across to the Mission bungalow, takes the large brass gong and beats it vehemently on the edge of the flat ground that lies in the front of the bungalow, thus calling all the schoolboys to file up, and there at the back of the Mission station on a level piece of ground they form a line. At seven o'clock sharp I myself go out to them, saluting them in military fashion, they at the same time saluting also. After this the head boy is given instructions what work each is to do, and they go away to their various duties with cheerful hearts, for from seven till nine all the schoolboys have to work on the compound.

Some are allotted off to weeding or to digging, to pruning plants, transplanting, making rockeries, collecting ferns and flowers from the jungle, and in this way the compound of the Mission Station is kept in civilized order, whilst their lessons in gardening, superintended the whole of the time by myself, are of great advantage to them, teaching them to care for the flowers and the beautiful plants which for generations their forefathers have trodden under foot without so much as a thought. No sooner had they been arranged in fancy beds and planted out and cared for in a proper manner, than the natives from far distant villages made their way up to the Mission Station in order to see the various specimens of plants which are set out in the garden, and the schoolboys have learned to take a great pride in this their work and have of their own accord named the Mission Station the "School Village."

Another group of boys are allotted off to care for

the pony, to fetch its food from the jungle, and also to look after the cows and the goats, and do likewise for them. Thus they learn how to look after their own domestic animals, and to take proper care of them, for the Lakhers possess a number of these domestic animals themselves, but if they die they die, if they live they live, and such a thing as properly stabling and properly feeding of these animals is foreign to them.

As soon as the two hours' work is completed, the head boy takes the large brass gong once again and beats it with all his might, probably with greater force than he did when calling them to work, and the boys all file away to the spring, 400 feet below the Mission Station, with a large cake of soap in their hands, and each boy has to bathe himself from head to foot every morning.

Half an hour is allowed for this work, and at 9.30 the gong is once more beaten and the boys file up into the school-house and take their places in rows, whilst I myself give out the hymn, offer prayer, and then school commences.

During the last year, however, the schoolboys themselves have opened the school every morning in turn, each boy taking his turn in rotation to give out the hymn and to pray, and in this way they have all been learning how to conduct their own meetings.

Prayers over, they start with their primers and their slates, some on their alphabet, others reading, others as far advanced as simple arithmetic, and we have taught these people to teach one another. Should a boy be doing simple words only, one who can read better than himself has to help him along, so as a rule they are allotted off two and two, and they do not learn in silence, but the hum of their voices the whole of the time is a strange feature of their mode of grasping knowledge, it greatly increases their ability to receive instruction, and so such a thing as silence in the school is unknown.

The most strange thing in my mind, however, is how they can learn one speaking against another the whole of the time. One boy will be reading over quite a different page to the boy that sits next to him, both of them talking out loud, and neither of them seeming to receive a word which the other has said, but all closely intent on their own business; and it is surprising to see with what speed these promising men can grip hold of and overcome the three R's.

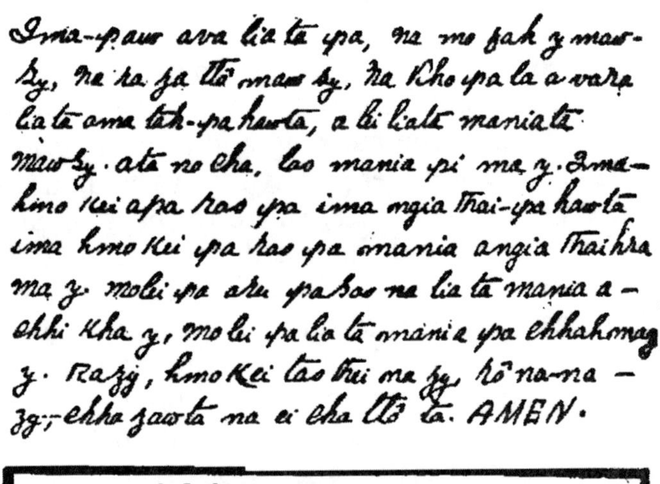

LAKHER PIONEER MISSION.
THE LORD'S PRAYER IN LAKHER WRITTEN BY A LAKHER SCHOOL-BOY AFTER ONLY ONE YEAR'S EDUCATION. 1911 ([illegible])

At twelve o'clock the gong is beaten again, and they leave school for an hour to play, or eat food, or do whatever they like. At one o'clock the gong sounds once more, and they re-enter school to go through the same performance until three or four o'clock according to the season of the year, when the gong sounds and the boys are free for the rest of the day.

In their home they live under our supervision. They cook their own food, they fetch their own water, they fetch their own wood, they do their own house cleaning, and as they have no beds but the bamboo mat, their bed arranging duties are not very arduous, rolling themselves up in their large sheets generally drawn right over their faces to save any stray mosquito from biting them or disturbing their slumbers; thus they lie peacefully until the morning breaks.

On Wednesday evenings we hold a service and singing class combined, then on Sundays Sunday-school is held in the morning and a meeting in the afternoon, and, weather permitting, we hold an open-air meeting in the village, where the boys all gather round in a circle and sing lustily the praises to God in their own tongue, whilst a hundred or more of the villagers will gather round and listen to a short Gospel Message, at which from time to time some one in the audience will ask many questions.

At these open air meetings not only our Lakhers are present, but the pigs and the fowls and the goats and the yelping curs of the village seem to love to congregate, and ofttimes make a great hubbub, much to the distraction of all concerned; at such times there is generally some kind soul who has some slight regard for our taxed energies, who with a log of wood drives the offending animals from the circle.

Every night round the fire in the schoolboys' dwelling-house, the schoolboys gather in a circle and hold on their own account a meeting, singing many hymns and offering up several prayers. This has been formed into quite a habit amongst them, and I have often listened to prayers uttered by these men which were simply and beautifully uttered, and whilst they do not profess to be Christians out and out, yet surely God Who loves them so dearly and Jesus Christ their Saviour Who gave His life that they might live, hears these prayers and accept them; and is it not true also that the heart of the Saviour is made to bound and the Angels in Heaven record the simple requests of these sons of head-hunters who are just being brought out from the darkness of heathenism into the Great and Glorious Light of the Gospel of Jesus Christ.

The work of the school is the backbone of the Mission. In it we have our hope of reaching every Tribe throughout the Lakher Country. Through it we have the hope of winning numbers of souls for Christ, and during the pioneer years of our sojourn amongst these people, from amongst those schoolboys two have come out definitely for the Saviour, throwing aside all their heathen devices of devil-appeasing worship, refusing to sacrifice to demons any longer, but trusting with their whole heart, with their whole life in the Redeeming Blood of the Saviour of mankind, believing that Christ has paid the pardon with His Precious Blood, and does no longer require the blood of beasts or fowls to cleanse from stain of sin.

The first boy to come out on the Lord's side was "Thytu," a lad of twelve years of age, and since he has made that decision his life has changed entirely. That decision was made on the 16th of September, 1910, and from that time forth he has been increasing day by day in knowledge and in light, and his life tells out in his endeavour to help others, a thing so foreign to the Lakher mind, that he is endeavouring to follow his Master and that the Holy Spirit is teaching him the Way of Life.

That was a glorious day for the Mission when, just as the sun had gone down and darkness was overspreading the earth, two boys came up together, one Thytu and one of the other boys, and according to the Lakher custom a man always speaks his wants through a third person, and in this case the other boy was commissioned to tell me that Thytu who was with him wanted to have his name enrolled on the Christian Register as a follower of the Lord Jesus Christ, the firstfruit of the Lakher Pioneer Mission, the first diamond in the rough to be chosen out, to be formed into the Likeness of the Blessed Saviour Himself.

I took the lad into my study, and there we had a long earnest talk together about all that it might mean to be a Follower of the Saviour, and asked him if he was willing even now to place his name upon the register. He had quite made up his mind to forsake his devil-appeasing worship, and to follow the One and Only True God, Jehovah, and to accept Jesus Christ as his Saviour and Master; and kneeling down together I commended him to God's care, and from that day forth his whole life has borne out the realities of the decision arrived at that evening.

Six months later we had the joy of another boy coming out from amongst our schoolboys. His name was "Chiahu," and although not such a bright lad as Thytu, yet he has endeavoured as far as he has received the Light to walk in that Light, and God has and will honour his endeavour.

When we see these two lads coming out on the Lord's side in the first few years of a pioneering venture, and when we think of all the possibilities that lie in the boys of our school, what an incentive it should be for each one of us to endeavour to press forward with full might and vigour, that the uttermost limits of Lakherland may be reached through the Gospel of Jesus Christ, and that His Kingdom may come and that the Strongholds of the Devil may fall and the Standard of Jehovah may fly on every pinnacle in that land.

When the boys go home on holiday they disperse to their various villages, there to hold their own meetings amongst their own kindred, to sing the praises of Jehovah in their own homes, to tell out once again the Wonderful Story of Salvation through Jesus Christ, to those to whom we at the present time are unable to reach, and in this way the knowledge of the Saviour is spread from village to village throughout the greater part of Lakherland.

One evening just at dusk I was accosted on my verandah by a band of some twelve Lakhers from a far-off village, and one of them said to me, " Pâpu, will you show us a picture of our Chief ? " I thought for a moment and could not understand what they were driving at, and said, " What picture of your Chief ? I haven't a picture of your Chief, who told you that I had ? " And then one of them, after fumbling through a number of sentences trying to explain what he wanted, said, " You know, Pâpu. I mean our Chief Jesus," and then I realized that he wished to see one of the Sunday School pictures which hung up in the school-house, the fame of which must have spread abroad, so I went in and fetched the picture.

It was one of Jesus Christ standing with His arms outstretched in a pleading way, whilst at the back was great darkness. There He stood as if pleading to those Lakhers to come unto Him, and it gave me a splendid opportunity of telling out once more, to those enquiring men, of the Love of God, of the sacrifice of Jesus Christ, of His Second Coming, and of His pleading that they should be followers of Him.

They must have stayed about an hour gazing at that picture, making many remarks amongst themselves, and after bidding me good-night they turned their faces towards the village.

The picture had been seen, the seed had been sown, the bread was cast upon the waters, may it be reaped after many days; and thus incident after incident of this kind of thing has come to our knowledge, one telling another and passing the Word along, preparing the way for the Gospel of Jesus Christ to enter into the hearts, to take captivity captive and set the prisoner free, snapping the bonds of sin, the chains of superstition and ignorance, making a clean sweep, leading the Tribes out of its heathen darkness to the Glorious Light of the Lord Jesus Himself.

CHAPTER XVI

THE LAKHER PRINCESS

PIONEERS in all the ages of the world have been men and women who have had to stand against much opposition from their fellow-men, and have had to face enormous odds in order to carry out their designs, and on this new pioneering venture my brave wife and myself found the odds ofttimes overwhelming, and had we been carrying it out in our own strength should certainly have failed absolutely.

But we were not pioneering the Lakhers with any self-centred object. Our one great theme was to carry out the Last Command of our Lord and Master, " Go ye into all the world and preach the Gospel to every creature," and with that command we had His great promise which can never fail, " Lo, I am with you alway, even unto the end." So here we were toiling from early morn until late at eve in labours of all sorts, preparing a home in which to live, providing for the needs of the body, seeking to relieve those that were in pain and affliction, snatching at every opportunity word after word of the language and noting it carefully down, endeavouring to point the people to the light which shines from the Cross. In peril of storms ; in peril of savage men ; in peril of sickness ; in fact, surrounded by a barrier of hardships which had to be overcome, but that promise, "Lo, I am with you alway," was a promise that ever ran through our minds, and in all those years of uphill pioneer work that promise ever proved faithful and true. Not in our strength but in His were we working; in His Name had we gone forth; and in His Name were we to conquer, and come out more than victors through Him that loved us.

The obstacles which had to be overcome were legion, but the two greatest obstacles that stood in our way were those of language and of gaining the confidence of these promising people, a savage race of head-hunters.

By His Grace and by His power the language obstacle had been overcome; the backbone of the language having been broken we had little to fear from that point from henceforth; but gaining the confidence of the whole of the tribes of Lakhers was another great obstacle which lay in front of us, and by works of love in attending to their sick, ministering to their wants, and by the great aid of my wife in helping to clothe the little ones with those warm coats, we were enabled to gain the confidence of the majority of the people; and yet there were numbers of the people who were opposed to our very residence in their country, and these too had to be won over in some way or other, but in our minds it seemed an impossibility. The more we tried to gain their confidence and respect the more bitter they appeared towards us. However, "God moves in a mysterious way, His wonders to perform," and in our case it was none the less a wonderful way in which the complete confidence of the people was won over to ourselves and to the Lakher Pioneer Mission.

Two years had passed away, when on September 18th, 1909, my wife presented me with a little daughter.

Far removed from all medical aid, from all civilized society, my brother kindly offered to come out from Lungleh to be with us during that time, and in company with his wife arrived as far as the opposite bank of the Kolodyne river, a little less than a day's journey from our bungalow, and there they were doomed to remain for three long days owing to the heavy rains that had swelled the Kolodyne to such an extent that it was impossible for any one to cross by boat or raft.

We in Sherkor watched anxiously the rise and fall of that river during those three days, and as soon as we saw the water was subsiding sufficiently to allow a safe passage, knowing that it was useless for them to attempt to swim their ponies across, we sent down our Mission pony to meet them, and in due course they arrived, tired out.

It was a joyful meeting, to be re-united once again after so long, and to be able to discuss the news with one another, but my brother's wife on arrival was feeling exceedingly out of sorts, having been so for some days past, and on the following morning she was unable to keep about, and had to take to her bed. Soon it was very evident that she was suffering with an attack of typhoid fever, and there for several days she lay getting weaker and weaker, my brother and my dear wife attending to her every want.

At last our expected happy event came to a reality, and after an exceedingly trying three days, during which we quite thought God would call my dear wife home to Himself and the joy which we had so long looked for would culminate in a great sorrow—my brother's wife also lying in a very sad condition in another room of the bungalow—a marvellous act of Providence gave to us the care of a little daughter, and a speedy restoration of her mother.

Does God direct? . . . Does God lead? . . . Does He care for the welfare of His children? . . . These questions are answered from the following little incident which is wonderful in its simplicity.

Previous to my brother leaving Lungleh to visit us, for some unknown reason he had quite accidentally, so far as this incident was concerned, written to the plains for a small bottle of a certain drug, thinking that it might come useful in his various medical duties, although never having used the drug himself before. When leaving his station to join ourselves, he fortunately placed this little bottle along with his luggage, without the slightest notion of any likelihood of using it, and therefore did not give it a thought. After over two days of great anxiety, and feeling that all our hopes of a safe delivery were fast dwindling away, as a drowning man clutching at a straw, after much prayer and examination I came to the conclusion that such and such was the matter.

On telling my brother he immediately took down the medical book from the shelf and opened the pages, when almost immediately his eyes fell on the details of such a possibility as I had suggested, a thing of which neither of us in all our studies had received any knowledge of before.

With this information a remedy was suggested, with the possible hope of a rectification, and the drug which was named was the very drug which my brother had quite accidentally placed amongst his goods.

He sprang up with great hope in his eyes,—as I write this I can see him now,—and eagerly searched through his native baskets to find this drug. Coming back with the precious bottle in his hand, he sat down at the dining-room table and very carefully weighed out the few grains that went to the dose, and then we administered it to my wife.

It acted like magic. For two days and a half she had had no rest, but it almost immediately sent her off to sleep. In twenty minutes' time the second dose was administered, and during those critical moments for us I was accosted by a large band of Lakhers, who called me out to argue some question or other which was not at that time at all congenial to me, but their real object no doubt was to obtain the latest news. We might say that they were the very enthusiastic news reporters for the country.

I, however, managed to rid myself of them, and made my way into the quiet room once again. It was an anxious time indeed, but God in His great Mercy caused that drug to carry out His will. It was the means, through His Grace, of not only saving the life of my dear wife, but of bringing into the world a daughter who was to seal the friendship of the Lakher Tribes with that of ours, and what was more, to cause them to heed more than ever before the Wonderful Story of the Saviour's Love for them.

The little one grew fast, and my wife made a speedy recovery and was up and about again in due course.

Never shall I forget my brother's loving help, sympathy, and sacrifice to me at this critical time, and we shall never forget the anxious time we had during those weeks together. Our dear wives lying sick, ourselves full of anxiety, our cows refusing sufficient milk to feed the invalids, and our goats also giving an exceedingly small quantity, all this making it doubly hard, but God in His wonderful mercy raised up both of our wives, and gave them back to us once again in full health and strength, for which we praise His Name and ever remember His mercies towards us. Does God answer prayer? . . . Does God care for His children? . . . Does He provide? . . . are fully answered in this little story of a little bottle full of a few little crystals which was bought most certainly through the Master's guiding hand and fore-knowledge of which was to come such an issue, not only to ourselves individually, but to the Lord's Work in that far-off corner of His vineyard.

The little one was not long to be held in seclusion. Lakhers teemed up to our bungalow to see the first white child that had ever been born in their country and the first white child which they had ever set eyes on.

Sherkor village arrived in full audience. People from every village round for many days' journey came up day by day to pay, as it were, their homage to the little one; and as we looked upon the scene our thoughts were turned to that scene which happened two thousand years ago of a Babe that was born in a manger in Bethlehem, where the shepherds and the wise men came to visit and to bring their gifts of love. These primitive people in their primitive way were paying similar respects to their new treasure, and little gifts of bananas, and cucumbers, and egg fruit, and such like were brought up in quite a large quantity for the child to play with.

Very soon it was evident that the little one was to bear, throughout life, the name and honour which they wished to confer on her in the rather lengthy name of "Tlôsai Zua Nô," and being translated means "The Lakher Princess," while there was nothing that pleased them more than when we told them that beside her two English names she was to have the name "Tlosai" (with the circumflex accent left out) added in commemoration of the people and country amongst whom and in which she was born, her full name thus being Louise Marguerite Tlosai Lorrain.

From that time forth both my wife and myself had natives' names, by which throughout the whole of that country we shall be known until the day when our names shall have disappeared from the knowledge of these peoples. My dear wife's name is "Tlôsai Nô," which being interpreted means "The Mother of the Lakher Princess," and my name was "Tlôsai Paw," which means "The Father of the Lakher Princess." In conferring this name upon the babe they indeed showed their kindly feelings towards us, and from that day forth the whole aspect of the work amongst these wild yet very interesting peoples has entirely changed, and we are able to breathe more freely an air of great friendship, even amongst those who had up to this time been so opposed to our residence amongst them, and who were now won over to kindly feelings and a brotherly sympathy. Before this they seemed to look upon us as somewhat differing from themselves; now, however, through the birth of a little child, they perceived that we too were human.

Day by day, as great numbers of natives came to

see the new-born babe, many very amusing questions were often asked concerning "Tlosai." One man in particular on one occasion came up to the bungalow and asked if he might see the little one, and after expressing his thoughts aloud he turned to us and asked us a question, saying, "Pâpu, my people say that 'You give Tlosai a large cake of food to eat, one meal off which without any further feeding can suffice her for two weeks, and that is why none of our people ever see your wife feeding the little one with rice as is our custom.' Now, is this true, or is it not?"

Of course I denied the statement, and then explained to him how it was that the little one was sustained entirely by the milk from its mother without any additional food whatever, with the consequence that she remained in perfect health and strength and was rapidly developing.

The reason for a Lakher asking such a question as this will be easily understood when one considers their mode of feeding infants, as before referred to, and the greatest wonder to them was the fact that not only was the "Tenth Day Fever" absent, but the little one developed with greater rapidity than their own infants, and what was more kept in perfect health and strength.

This, therefore, gave us a wonderful opportunity of showing them how practical it was to bring a baby up in a natural way, and enabled us to drive home with great force what we had been continually teaching them in years past, for wherever this rice feeding of babies has been stopped this fever on the tenth day has never appeared, and if we could only get more of the Lakher women to bring up their children in a natural way the number of infantile

LOUISE MARGUERITE TLOSAI LORRAIN (age 3 years),
daughter of the Author and called by the Natives the "Lakher Princess"
(p. 245).

[To face p. 246.

deaths would be exceedingly reduced and the poor little things would be saved an enormous amount of suffering as well.

It may not be known to my reader, but all the same it is a fact, that when a native baby is born it is not black but red, and in the course of a few days this redness will turn to darkness. There is, of course, a difference between a native new-born babe and the new-born babe of a white man, but still that difference is not very great during the first few days of existence, and one of the problems which the Lakhers wished to solve, believing that we held the secret, was how we managed to keep our babies white and save them from turning black. They thoroughly believed that we practised some kind of witchcraft, or gave them some special medicine in order to bring about this condition, and time after time we were asked to tell them the secret in order that they too might keep their babies white, and we found this a splendid opportunity of suggesting to them that the very best method they could adopt was to use soap and water more freely day by day, for the Lakhers are naturally exceedingly dirty as before mentioned.

Another question which was asked us from time to time was—Would the Government seize Tlosai and send her away to England, for they had heard rumoured that whenever a white child was born in this part of the world the Government would not allow them to remain there, but immediately caused them to be sent to their own country, and they were not at all sure or certain that they would be able to have Tlosai among them for very long, until I assured them that she would remain with her parents, the Government having no control whatever over her, and this statement seemed to calm their fears greatly.

After the birth of Tlosai and the restoration to health of both my brother's wife and my own, the time at last arrived for my brother and his wife to take their journey back to Lungleh once again, and before leaving we had a service at which Tlosai was dedicated to the service of the Lord, along with an expression of thankfulness to our loving Heavenly Father Who had given us the company and helpful services of my brother, and for a joyful passing out of all the trials and difficulties which we all had been passing through, and dedicating ourselves more fully to His service in the salvation of the Lushai and Lakher tribes.

Bidding my wife farewell from the compound, and accompanied by a native I went with them two miles into the jungle, and then coming to the brow of a steep hill, with a farewell and a prayer on our lips to God for all His Mercy and a safe journey to my two loved ones back to their country, they passed into the jungle which soon hid them from sight, and once again I turned my face towards our lonely homestead to plod on with the enlargement of the hymn-book, to finish the dictionary, to complete the translation of St. John's Gospel, and to carry on our now large school of Lakher tribesmen, that the name of Jesus might be known throughout the length and breadth of the land, believing that one day we shall see the whole of Lakherland under the reign of the King of Kings.

CHAPTER XVII

BACK TO CIVILIZATION

THE work at the Mission Station had now grown to such an extent that the days did not seem long enough to complete all that had to be done within the hours available.

Shortly after five in the morning saw us astir, and no sooner had one left their bed-chamber than the duties of the day pressed hard upon one. Patients came to our dispensary to obtain relief from their many ills or to obtain relief for some friend of theirs who was lying on a sick-bed in a distant village, while numbers of Lakhers from over the border outside Government jurisdiction frequented our dispensary for the same purpose and found in our remedies great relief, and through our medical work we have been able to get into touch with almost every Chief and vast numbers of the common people who are situated far from our district in distant parts where the Government will not allow us at the present time to penetrate.

Although the penetration into these far distant villages of the Lakhers across the border is forbidden by Government, yet we have gradually been able to come into contact with these people, and whilst caring for their bodies have been enabled to preach the Unsearchable Riches of Christ, and tell them of One Who loved and loves them dearly even to the sacrifice of Himself; so that at the present day it matters not how far one may penetrate into the Lakher country, our names have become known, and in a greater number of cases not only our names but ourselves are known personally, which in the years to come will prove invaluable to the spread of the Gospel in these far distant outlying villages.

The pressure of work was very great upon us, having twenty-two Lakher tribesmen in our school to care for, to look after, to control and to educate, and these of necessity took up the greater part of the day, whilst continual interruption for medical work greatly curtailed the time at our disposal.

The dictionaries of the language, too, were now on the point of completion,—two dictionaries having been compiled, each containing between seven and eight thousand references apiece. The first dictionary was a Lakher-English, while the second was an English-Lakher dictionary, and a complete grammar of the language also was now completed.

Our hymn-book of thirty-seven selections proved inadequate to the present demand, and we were bound to enlarge it to sixty-eight selections, the completion of which was much appreciated by those in our school.

Our "Questions and Answers on God's Plan of Salvation from Genesis to Revelation" had been learned by heart by the greater number of the boys at the school, and it proved an invaluable help to their grasping an all round knowledge of the Word of God and helping them to understand their St. John's Gospel, which they had themselves been writing out in their own handwriting, in a more intelligent manner.

The Primer, which the Assam Government had kindly printed for the Mission free of charge, proved a useful adjunct to our work, and by its means a number of the Lakhers outside of the school started to learn some of the mysteries of reading and writing themselves, being aided by the schoolboys themselves during their spare time, whilst as the sun sank in the west one would often hear the swelling of Christian hymns from one Lakher hut and another throughout the village of Sherkor, several of the schoolboys having gone down with the express purpose of teaching some of the maidens and young men the words of the hymns, and thus distributing the truths that they contain, and this brings us into an optimistic view of the future of the Lord's Work through the instrumentality of the Lakher Pioneer Mission amongst these most interesting and wild hillsmen.

The Lakher tribesman enters the Mission school for a period of twelve months' training, during which time he acquires a thorough grounding in the fundamentals of Christianity and Christian living, coming under the influence of a Christian home and Christian surroundings, cut off from all his heathen rites and ceremonies during that time.

The time comes when these men and boys have their annual holiday, and they immediately depart for their various villages, not, however, to lay aside the work which they have been doing during the past months, but they go as forerunners of the Gospel of Jesus Christ, for on their arriving at their villages their fellow-villagers are very keen on hearing the latest news, and immediately their books are brought forth and with a sense of pride, perhaps, at being able to read and write, showing their superiority to even their betters in rank who have not yet unravelled the mysteries of the Three R's, they tell forth the simple story of the Cross, singing the Christian hymns and teaching their fellow-villagers the same, whilst they are plied with question upon question dealing with God, the Lord Jesus, the Devil and the Great Beyond, and they are proud to be able to meet these questions with a reasonable answer; and thus through our school work not only the number of boys and men which comprise our school are being reached with the Gospel of Jesus Christ, but they themselves are permeating the whole country with the truth which is so precious to every Christian heart, preparing the way for the Missionary and preparing the hearts of the people for a full and free Salvation in the near future.

Whilst five years ago the name of Jesus Christ had never been uttered in the Lakher language, and never a hymn of joy sung in that tongue, only the old heathen dirges,—for Christianity alone brings the song of joy,—yet in so short a space of time as five years the Lord has wonderfully blessed the endeavour put forward in answer to a Divine Call, in response to His Command, that through a great part of the Lakher country many a hill top to-day is resounding with the Praises of Jehovah, and a slight knowledge of Jesus Christ as our Lord and King, the Saviour and Redeemer of the Lakhers, has probably reached to the remotest villages of Lakherland, and it is very probable that there is not a village throughout the length and breadth of the country where there are not some of its inhabitants who have heard the Gospel story, either direct from the Missionary himself or else through

Lakher men at their national sport of wrestling.

Teaching in a Lakher Village (*p.* 207).

[*To face p.* 252.

the medium of the tribesmen who have come within the influence of the Lakher School.

For the last two years we have been bound to work at high pressure, rising soon after five in the morning and seldom seeing our bed before the hour of midnight had struck, for the burden of the language was very great upon my brain, and no rest could be obtained until all the work of the day had been entered up, in order that the dictionaries and the Gospel of St. John should not lag behind, whilst my dear wife worked in the glow of the oil lamp at providing the children with coats and the schoolboys with shirts to keep them from feeling the fall in temperature, and in endeavouring to create in them some slight appreciation of refinement and cleanliness, for seldom did she leave the work until I myself had completed the day's task, however late that might be.

Single-handed as we were with the pressure of an ever-growing work, it would have been impossible for us to have accomplished the whole of the work which we set ourselves, by the grace of God, to undertake, had we not burned the midnight oil during six days in the week.

But God blessed the labours of our hands and gave to us our hearts' desire, and has honoured our labours by allowing us to give to the Lakhers not only their language in writing and in seeing the first-fruits of the Gospel brought to the Foot of the Cross, but He has honoured us by giving to ourselves that peculiar honour of placing in the hands of the Lakhers the first portion of the precious Gospel which we trust may be the means of drawing many to Him that they may be converted and live, and in their turn tell forth the glorious tidings of Salvation through Jesus Christ, reaching to the remotest parts of their country where it may be impossible for the white man to penetrate for many years to come.

Well do I remember the nights when the manuscript of the Gospel according to St. John was completed, and when my hand had penned the last words of the dictionaries, how, catching them up in my hands, I threw them up in the air, catching them again and crying "Hoorah! the task is completed," and my wife, with myself, rejoiced to know that God had given to us the victory over all the seeming unsurmountable difficulties that four years previously we were called to face.

* * * * *

At last the day dawned when we were to bid the little Lakher Pioneer Mission Station farewell for a furlough in the Homeland, and for days past we had been busy packing away our goods in boxes and trunks and fixing up our loads for the journey, filling them with the bare necessities of the march, and 4 a.m. saw us out of bed and making ready the loads for the carrier who were to bear our goods across the hills.

When we arrived in the country it was almost impossible to get any one to work for us, and I had rather doubted how we should fare for carriers at this time, but to our joy we found more men had come in for loads than we had ever anticipated, and so that difficulty was removed from us, for we found that many more wished to see us on our journey as far as possible, and to bid us a short farewell, than we were aware of.

Thylai, Chief of Sherkor, was up at our bungalow that morning long before the sun was up, and there he, with a number of other head-men of the village, remained sitting on the level piece of ground outside the bungalow until noon, when we were ready to start. The poor old man was over seventy years of age, and he was very much unnerved at the thought of our leaving him, and it made us feel sorry to see the poor old man nearly crying. His affection for our little daughter " Tlosai " appeared great, and his one theme was " You will bring her back again, won't you ? "

The great attachment these people have to our little daughter has, I feel sure, been one of the greatest factors in making the Lakher tribesmen and ourselves friends, and will in the future, I am certain, be one of the greatest levers in helping them to decide for Christ and to leave all their demon worship.

The old Chief accompanied by quite a band of men and women, many of whom had at the commencement of our Mission been exceedingly opposed to our residence in the country, followed us down to the outskirts of the village and bade us a last farewell, and the man who had been the ringleader of those prejudiced against us, and whose name was " Va-tlai," was one of the foremost in begging us to return again amongst them; and after bidding them all farewell and assuring them that if God spared us, both my wife, Tlosai, and myself would return to them after a furlough in the Homeland, we made our way into the jungle and Sherkor village was lost to sight.

* * * * *

The story of our journey home is a long one, and cannot be recorded here, but in due course after a journey of three months all but four days, we arrived in the Homeland, for it must be remembered that when we left Sherkor we had before us practically a month's journey before we reached civilization.

After our arrival in the Homeland, one of the things that struck us most was to find how many Faithful Souls had been holding us up in Prayer daily during all our adventuresome travels and pioneering trials in Lakherland, and then we were able to realize to some little extent how it was that power had been given to ourselves to accomplish the Will of the Master, and to overcome all the numerous difficulties in the far-off Regions Beyond.

We had brought home with us in manuscript the work of the past years, and the Gospel according to St. John in the Lakher language has been accepted by the British and Foreign Bible Society, who have now printed it for the Lakher Pioneer Mission, and whilst I am penning these lines the precious volumes are on their way to Calcutta and thence to the field. To Him Who gave the strength and the grace to complete the work which Angels might well envy, be all Glory, Honour and Praise.

The Lakher Pioneer Mission was launched in faith in answer to a Divine call, and throughout the years of its existence has been much hampered for funds, but God in His Mercy knew the needs and has shown forth from time to time His power in supplying for His servants, and throughout all the years the Mission has not been financed by any one individual, but has been carried on through the sympathies for the greater part of friends and co-workers whose human form it has never been our pleasure to behold.

There is one helper, however, amongst our numerous friends, whose Christian help and enormous sacrifices on behalf of the Salvation of the Lakhers commands a mention here, and whilst the name may not be mentioned, yet God knows, and we know of the great self-sacrifices that have been made from time to time, and these have been a great stimulus to my beloved wife and myself in times of trial, temptation and hardship, and have urged us to endeavour to make the work which the Lord had seen fit to place in our hands worthy of that self-sacrifice and love for Him and His cause.

Whilst we have been favoured with the honour of going forward into the field in the name of the Master, all praise and honour be given to those who have loyally held the ropes in the Homeland both with their valued prayers and pecuniary help, and especially is our thanks due to the Honorary Secretary, Miss May G. Laidlaw, and to the Honorary Treasurer, Mr. J. W. Macdonald, who have so loyally attended to the accounts of the Lakher Pioneer Mission in the Homeland during the past years.

Whilst the Primer in the Lakher language has been so kindly printed by the Assam Government for the Mission free of charge, yet at the present time we hold the two dictionaries of the language, together with the grammar, the hymn-book of sixty-eight selections, and the Story of God's Plan of Salvation still in manuscript, and which we had hoped to have passed through the press during our furlough. Up to the present time no friend has been found to meet the expenses of these productions, but we trust that ere long some one will be forthcoming to place these most valuable works in the hands of the Lakhers, to the Glory and Honour of our Lord and Master, and to the uplifting of the Lakher Tribes.

The work of the Lakher Pioneer Mission has been for God, for the extension of the Empire of His Son, our Lord and Master Jesus Christ, and for the glory of our own beloved Empire, in endeavouring to bring into a wild country, and amongst a still wilder people, the seeds of Peace, while endeavouring to cause all misunderstandings to be cleared away by the means of a clear understanding of their native tongue, manners, customs, religious rites and ceremonies, and thus giving the authorities of our Empire a firm and righteous hold over the people, and causing justice to be meted out in righteousness and fairness and to the satisfaction of both ruler and ruled, that the floating of the Union Jack upon the borders of that land may stand as an ensign to the Lakhers for Liberty, Justice and Peace.

May God in His Mercy grant to these chocolate-coloured tribes in Lakherland a future that shall be grander and more noble through the Power of the Gospel of our Lord and Master Jesus Christ, that when He comes, as we believe He soon will, every tribe through the Lakher Hills may flock to His Standard and exclaim—

> I am on the Lord's side,
> Saviour, I am Thine.

* * * * *

There is an adage which says: "The mill will not grind with the water that is passed," and we must ask ourselves faithfully the question: "What about the future of these Lakher tribes, what are the needs and what are our plans?"

At the very outset of the proposed Mission to the Lakhers, the Treasurer received the following letter from Lieut.-Col. John Shakespear, British Resident at Manipur :—

The Residency,
Manipur, Assam.
23rd August, 1905.

My Dear Sir,

I have received the little paper about the Lakher Pioneer Mission, and am very glad to hear that this tribe is about to have the benefit of a Mission of their own, especially as a brother of my old friend, Mr. J. Herbert Lorrain, is to conduct it.

I am particularly interested in the Lakhers, as I was the first to explore their country and to take it over on behalf of the British Government. To be accurate, I should say to take over a part of their country, for the Lakher villages extend to a considerable distance beyond our border. The Lakhers are not the original inhabitants of the country they now inhabit, but are immigrants from the Chin Hills. They are less intelligent than the Lushais, and less anxious to be educated, but when they have a Sahib of their own I feel sure they will progress. The Lakher villages, which are administered from Lungleh, are rather difficult to get at from that place, and their dialect being different, they have not received the same amount of attention as the Lushai inhabitants of the district, but I feel sure that Mr. Reginald A. Lorrain will find them pleasant people to work amongst. Your remarks as to the danger of these Hill tribes becoming Hinduised is very real, and Manipur is an instance in point. The Manipuris have become Hindus within historical times, and are more bigoted than the highest Brahmins of Hindustan. The result is such as to make it incumbent on every one who has the interests of the Hill people at heart, irrespective of his own religious views, to exert himself to prevent other tribes becoming Hinduised.

If I can be of any use in supplying information I shall be glad to answer any questions sent me.

* * * * *

Wishing you all success in the work,
I remain, yours faithfully,
(*Lieut.-Col.*) *JOHN SHAKESPEAR.*

Seven years have passed away since the receipt

of the above letter, and five years of work completed in the field, and now the country lies before us, the door has been opened, and it behoves every follower of the Lord Jesus Christ to see that the door is never closed again until the King of Glory has entered in.

There is a great work before us, a great responsibility, a stupendous task, but He is Faithful that promised, " Lo, I am with you alway, even unto the end."

The field is large, the labourers are few. Another labourer and his wife are required for the work, and funds to meet the ever-increasing work of the Lakher Pioneer Mission.

A school of a hundred Lakher tribesmen, I believe, could easily be organized were the funds forthcoming, and for each of these scholars the small sum of £3 a year to provide them with their food would be required.

The Pioneer Mission bungalow at the present time is practically destroyed by white ants and new buildings are required of a more permanent character, but not of an exorbitant nature, but suitable for habitation.

A school-house also to meet the needs of the school must be erected, and a dwelling-house for the schoolboys to live in must also come under consideration.

The following letter received from Lieut.-Col. G. H. Loch of the Indian Army, who is stationed at Aijal, North Lushai Hills, India, a distance of fifteen days' journey from our Mission Station at Sherkor, was visiting our part of the country at the beginning of 1911, while his first visit being at the very commencement of our work, before our Bungalow building was completed in 1907.

The letter below will speak for itself as the candid opinion of a British Official who knows the Lakher people and country, and whose words should help us all to put forth our utmost energy and consecration in the uplifting of these people:—

Lushai Hills,
April 18th, 1911.

My Dear Mr. Lorrain,

You ask me to write something about my impressions of your Mission at Sherkor since my last visit, and I gladly do so.

Three years ago, as you will remember, I passed through Sherkor for the first time on my way south to Tuipang, when the Column that was proceeding south to Zongling Village to punish them for their accumulated offences against our own people, was concentrating. You were at that time very much in the "pioneer" stage, and are so now for that matter—though there is a good deal of difference apparent between that time and this.

At that time, I will confess from what I had previously seen of the Lakhers, I came to the conclusion that a more unpromising type of people to work amongst as a Missionary, could hardly be conceived. They were, I think, the most indolent people I had ever come across. The Lushais were paragons of industry compared to them. I do not blame the Lakhers for their laziness if they can live and thrive without being industrious—but I mention it, as amongst such people Mission work does not involve the preaching of the Gospel only, but brings with it necessary, wholesome work for the Mission, in fact the gospel of honest work as well.

The Lakhers are a self-contained people, with few wants that cannot be satisfied from within, and if the Mission is also self-contained and can do such work as the erection of school buildings, etc., without outside assistance, so much the better for the Mission.

This year, when I visited the Mission, you had seventeen boys in the school, twelve of whom, you told me, could read and write well; and that some of them could manage simple arithmetic; the remainder were still in the preliminary stages with their primers. One thing that struck me was the beautiful hand-writing; better I should say than most English boys of a similar age, and with far greater opportunities, were capable of doing. I had much pleasure in hearing your school boys sing, which they did very well; they seem to have a natural aptitude for this, as indeed their neighbours the Lushais, also have. What you need now, is some instrument on which to accompany them.

I was glad to see, too, that most of the boys were cleanly turned out, and took some pride in being so. I put cleanliness next to Godliness for the people of these hills, and have always held that the more we impress upon them the necessity of being clean, the greater their self-respect; and once this is attained, other things will assuredly follow.

I noticed the absence of girls in your classes. I suppose it is too soon yet, in the history of your Mission; but I am confident that, with your wife, who knows the language so well, and who is so sympathetically inclined towards the people, it must be the wish of both of you that girl students will come in time.

If we are really to improve the home surroundings of these hill tribes, we must educate the women and work through them.

Women may not have, in these hills, the same influence amongt the community or in family life that they possess in more civilized countries, but I am confident that the more we civilize and raise the status of the women, the better the condition of the people will be, both from a material and moral point of view.

The Dispensary in connection with your Mission should prove to be a great factor in its success. There is nothing that these hill people appreciate more than medical treatment. They are without any remedies, even of the most simple kinds themselves and a great deal of suffering can be obviated by timely and comparatively simple treatment. As you know, the Government provide Dispensaries, and the medical officers in charge treat a very large number of cases; but there is certainly room for their work being supplemented by medical aid from Missionaries; especially is this true as regards villages remote from our stations. From the numbers you now treat (126 cases in January, 1911), I should say that you will find this branch of your Mission will rapidly expand.

I am glad to hear that your Lakher dictionary is progressing, and that your Grammar of the language is completed. I presume that you can arrange for the printing of the Lakher translation of St. John's Gospel, and the Catechism on "The substance of the Bible."

Looking at it all round, I think that your Mission may fairly be said to be past its most difficult stage; and, although there may be disappointments ahead, still with perseverance and tact, I feel confident that these will be overcome.

The one need of your Mission is buildings of a more permanent character, less liable to be damaged by the weather and more of an object lesson, once they are constructed, to the people amongst whom you live. The better ordered, the cleaner and the more "pucka" your Mission buildings, the greater the lesson they will silently teach. All this I know, means money; but this should be forthcoming once your appeal to those at home, able and willing to give, is made known.

Believe me, Yours sincerely,

G. H. LOCH, Lieut.-Col., Indian Army.

During the coming years, if the Lord spares us, it is our desire to visit every Lakher village that we can possibly obtain entrance to, and to hold in the village for several days at a time a Mission at which men and women will be taught to learn their alphabet, as well as the regular religious services and lantern lectures, hymn-books and primers being distributed, and prizes of small gifts being offered for those who learn to read and write a little.

In this way I believe it possible to claim the greater part of Lakherland for Christ. A slight knowledge of reading and writing once instilled in the mind of a Lakher man or woman will immediately cause a desire to spring up to further that knowledge with the speedy result of a clear knowledge of these arts, thus enabling a greater part of the Lakhers to read for themselves the Word of God, and for the Holy Spirit Who has promised to be our teacher to lead them into all truth.

These results cannot be accomplished save by the loyal followers of the Lord Jesus Christ cooperating together in this land to help us who are placed in the front of the fight.

Consecrated lives, consecrated prayers, consecrated purses are what are needed, and if we have this, Lakher heathenism will in a few years be a thing of the past, and every hill top throughout Lakherland from the North to the South, from the East to the West will resound with the Praise of Jehovah from hundreds and probably thousands of Redeemed lips of men, women and children, who are at this present time deep in superstition and sin, without a hope, without a Saviour, but who are BOUGHT with the PRICE of the SAVIOUR'S BLOOD, and who are but waiting for the Lord's servants in this land to send forth the Saving Knowledge of the Power of the Gospel unto Salvation in Christ Jesus until He come.